# AI FOR EDUCATORS

EMBRACE NEW TECHNOLOGIES TO ENRICH
CURRICULUM, IMPROVE TEACHING METHODS,
REDUCE BURNOUT, AND SAVE TIME AND ENERGY
WITH STRATEGIES THAT WORK

DANIELLE AUSTEN

# CONTENTS

# INTRODUCTION

Echoing throughout the tiled floors and whiteboard-clad walls of the classroom I've stood at the front of for over 25 years, the air is abuzz with an energy that's simply electric. Kids shuffle in and out, backpacks in tow, all chatting about the new viral TikTok trend or the latest phone they want to get.

As a lifelong advocate for and provider of education, today I find myself at a pivotal point in my career, managing the daily challenge of connecting with 30-plus tech-savvy but digitally unweaned students who are glued to their screens at all times, and who are also newly armed with powerful AI tools, to both their detriment and advantage.

Today's school-age kids didn't just grow up passively observing the internet, and the powerful technology that comes with it in its fully realized state; rather, they are *of* this age and are intimately tied to a technologically minded existence. I've always been a firm advocate of digital tools being funneled to students in useful ways that empower them and improve their prospects, rather than provide distractions, of which there are already far too many. The tools we have access to today as educators are simply mind-boggling.

Each student I have represents just one tiny pixel amid a broad spectrum of diverse learning styles and needs, creating a vast challenge for today's educators, but also a huge area for technology to improve tailored, individualized learning. Let's face it: The daunting task of tailoring lessons to meet every student's individual needs while navigating the complex curriculum requirements and policies set by school boards and administrators can be one of the more challenging aspects of our noble, yet notably under-compensated profession.

This isn't just an American problem, but rather a struggle faced by educators worldwide, each facing their own set of unique challenges. The statistics on the domestic front paint a vivid portrait of our shared challenges worldwide. According to the Brookings Institute, the student-teacher ratio in American public schools is 15:3 (Chingos & Whitehurst, 2011). This number is indicative of the uphill battle American educators face in providing the personalized attention each student deserves.

We, as dedicated educators, stand at the forefront of these issues today, and in doing so, too often struggle with burnout, limited resources, and student engagement challenges on top of it all. So, I ask you, dear reader, why did *you* pick up this book? What catalyzed your decision to explore the vast possibilities of AI in education?

Perhaps it was the relentless pursuit of effective teaching methods for your classroom despite all these challenges. Maybe it was that longing for more time and less stress, and the yearning to make a meaningful difference in the lives of our students that many of us have. Whatever the reason, I'm here for you, and I hear your frustration.

As we start to peer into the promising hands-on interactive tools that AI offers passionate educators like us, we can easily see that there are a number of great shortcuts that promise to reshape the educational landscape, from lesson planning to increasing classroom engagement. This guide to the vast possibilities AI represents isn't just a dry, theoretical exploration of the technology, but rather, is based on concrete analysis and actionable tips, providing you with a practical roadmap for improving your overall teaching experience.

In the pursuit of effective personalized learning, I myself have already discovered the power of AI tools, and now I'm here to serve as your seasoned guide, as I share these revelations with you. These tools have become my trusted virtual aids, helping me craft highly personalized education plans that address the unique needs and can even assist in mapping the progress of each student. The result: You can look forward to increased engagement and a deeper understanding of what your classroom is telling you.

AI apps, primarily chat-based large language models (LLMs), have become invaluable allies of mine. They automate the tedious administrative tasks that often consume my time, from organizing lessons to putting homework and study guides together. Liberated from these burdens, I find myself with the precious commodity of time—time to focus on teaching, connecting with my students, and crafting a more meaningful educational experience.

In my efforts to uncover strategies for enhanced student engagement, I've learned to wield AI as a tool for creating interactive and engaging learning environments. Incorporating these tools into the classroom isn't just about using technology for the sake of technology—it's about using it strategically to foster improved focus and participation. The classroom has the potential to become a dynamic, interactive space where technology enhances the learning experience rather than being a distraction.

What I've found is that AI can also represent a great strategy for future-proofing my teaching, as I now regularly gain insights by having my finger on the pulse of upcoming trends in educational AI. My conscious effort to stay tuned in to these new developments allows me to stay ahead in an ever-shifting, dynamic technological landscape, and has empowered me to be more aware of what emerging technologies could be of use in an educational context.

This emerging technology isn't just a promise for the future, as I'll show you throughout these pages; it's a reality for educators who have already embraced the power of AI. Throughout this book, you'll encounter a number of real-life case studies and teacher chatter from message boards that serve to illustrate the real potential found in these strategies. This book is far from a comprehensive, theoretical, pedagogical framework; rather, it's a practical reader-friendly guide based on real experiences and real results.

This isn't just another book about the much-hyped subject of AI, it's the *right* book for you. As you read through these pages, I'd like to invite you to close the gap between where you are now and where you want to be once the next academic year rolls around. I feel your pain and struggles in the classroom and can assure you that the only way to work past these hiccups is to start looking forward. It's time to take a tour of the educational tools of the future, steeping yourself in a vision that promises a better, more efficient, and fulfilling teaching experience for educators at all levels.

So, are you ready to start scrutinizing, and then begin gradually transforming your time-tested teaching methods to keep up with the rapid-fire technological progress of the future? It can be tough, but I promise you it will be rewarding. Let's jump right in and start exploring the practical world of AI for educators!

# PART I

## WHAT IS AI?

# 1

# WELCOME TO AI

**M**any people, especially fellow educators I know, hear the acronym AI and think something along the lines of: *bleggghhh! This buzzword I've been hearing everywhere is literally driving me crazy! My students use it to cheat, it's not reliable, it's not original, it's not up to date. What use is it to me?*

Well, they might not realize it, but around 77% of people (Hryshkevich, 2022) utilize AI-powered services in one way or another every single day. There's a prevalent notion that each one of us can make a concerted effort to actively avoid using AI, but this assumption is based on the fact that few people truly understand exactly what AI encompasses.

Let's take for example some of the commonly used technologies we rely on every day, such as voice assistants, map navigation, facial recognition, and smart devices. These common apps and features of the devices we use all rely on the power of AI to simplify quotidian tasks, and to make things easier for us.

If you use Siri, Alexa, or smart thermostats in your house, you're using AI. These so-called Internet of Things (IoT) devices aren't anywhere near the only AI-based tools you encounter when doing basic tasks. With automated personal and public transport just around the corner, and a vast range of applications in fields ranging from manufacturing to medicine, AI has arrived. This reality makes it all the more important to start learning more about what it is, and how it will continue to affect our lives.

Once we start to learn more about what it offers, only then can we begin to truly unpack and demystify this powerful technology. Once we understand the fundamentals behind the technology, we can then start to design our own custom use cases around it. As will become glaringly clear by the end of this book, AI actually *can* be utilized in helpful ways, including in administrative tasks, and in streamlining your teaching.

## WHAT IS AI?

If you close your eyes when you think about AI and you start picturing robots humming away in some kind of number-crunching laboratory, you're not wrong. But there's more to it than machines processing data. Harnessing the power of AI is like suddenly gaining access to an auxiliary brain that powers machines. These machines, in turn, can help us execute various tasks. While you can program a robot to help you clean your house, like a Roomba vacuum, you can't ask it questions, or ask it to do any task other than what it was designed for. This is where AI differs from the related fields of automation and robotics.

Here's where AI proves its merit within this spectrum of automated technology: It can be considered a flexible, adaptable, and trainable tool that can be used for a wide variety of generative tasks, including for tasks of automation. Consider how useful apps like Grammarly already use a programmed understanding of spelling and grammar to help editors edit, or to assist English teachers in quickly grading papers. While Grammarly itself is not an AI-based technology, the company has begun to offer a number of useful generative AI tools to complement its main product, such as an AI-powered writing assistant.

You've undoubtedly heard of ChatGPT. This large language model (LLM) chat-based tool can answer your queries, help you organize lists and written information, and can even compose letters and documents. The way these large language models work is through data training processes, where they're essentially fed information by their developers. What this means, however, is that these powerful language model engines are of course subject to any kind of inherent biases in the data they're trained on. Some of them can even access the internet independently, and as we educators know, the internet can be filled with vast amounts of unreliable or biased information.

AI also comes into play with recommendation algorithms. The music-streaming app Spotify, for example, uses AI to recommend music you might like. The more you listen to songs through the app, the more data the software collects about your tastes and preferences. It can then take that data, process it, and recommend songs for you based on your most-played tracks, helping you discover new artists. This approach to using AI to power technology that helps better connect people with their interests is similar to "Recommended for You" and "You Might Also Like" suggestions on Amazon and Goodreads.

Now that we've explored the more practical side of how you've undoubtedly already seen AI applied to today's commonly used products and services, let's jump into looking at the more technical side of the various types of algorithms behind the technology.

- **Machine Learning (ML)**: Machine learning trains computers to learn and extrapolate from pools of data. The goal is to have it make predictions or decisions without being explicitly programmed to have any particular output. The science of machine learning is based on training algorithms to recognize patterns and improve their performance over time.
- **Deep Learning (DL)**: Deep learning is a type of machine learning that uses artificial neural networks (ANNs) to solve complex mathematical problems. These neural networks are called "deep" because they have a layered architecture that's inspired by the complicated structure of the human brain's synapses and nodes. This technology is often employed in image and speech recognition, which often comes into use with self-driving cars and medical imaging.

- **Natural Language Processing (NLP)**: NLP focuses on getting algorithms to understand, interpret, and generate human language. This is the AI behind LLM-based chatbots, AI-fueled language translation apps, and voice assistants like Siri or Alexa. NLP helps machines communicate with us in a more natural, human-like way.
- **Robotics**: Robotics AI controls automated machines or equipment, allowing them to perform tasks or make decisions in the physical world. Examples include robots used in manufacturing, or military drones that can fly autonomously, utilizing AI to navigate and strike their targets.
- **Expert Systems**: Expert systems are AI programs specifically designed to mimic human expertise in a particular industry. They solve problems and make decisions based on rules and knowledge provided by experts who helped code and train them. You see these in areas like medical diagnosis and financial planning.

One of the best ways to conceptualize how AI can help us educators is by considering the example of Google searches. If you and I both search for the same term on Google right now, we'd get different results. That's because Google knows what I've searched for in the past and will use that information to curate my results, and it does the same for you.

The search algorithm uses AI to learn about us and analyze that data to deliver a personalized online experience, including pushing content such as news articles and advertisements that are curated toward our preferences, and anticipate our needs and expectations. If AI can do that for search results and customized ads, imagine how it can benefit your students!

## HISTORY OF AI

The term "artificial intelligence" dates all the way back to the mid-20th century. In 1950, British mathematician and computer scientist Alan Turing published "Computing Machinery and Intelligence." This paper introduced what we now call the "Turing Test," a notorious theoretical experiment that pitted man against machine.

The basic premise for how the test works is that a human judge engages in conversation with a machine. After following a specific set of criteria, if they still can't tell whether they're talking to a person or a computer, then the machine has successfully demonstrated human-like intelligence. While some AI engines have come close, to this date, none of them have successfully passed the Turing Test.

In the 1960s, AI became more popular as researchers and institutions developed computer programs that simulated human reasoning and problem-solving. Some of these programs would solve algebra problems, translate language, and even play chess with humans, most notably culminating decades later with IBM's Deep Blue defeating World Chess Champion Gary Kasparov in 1997 (Greenemeier, 2017).

That victory inspired researchers to turn their attention to AI once again, improving algorithms to power search engines and social media as the internet became more commonplace. In 2011, IBM's Watson competed and won on an episode of the quiz show *Jeopardy!*, showing the public how much natural language processing (NLP) could benefit humans (Walsh, 2021).

In recent years, the use of AI assistants like Siri and Alexa has become prevalent, and Tesla has launched self-driving cars that are trained using DL computer vision techniques.

Despite all the positive advancements, many news stories about AI are negative. Regular people, AI researchers, and business leaders alike have expressed concern about the ethical considerations and social ramifications of the powerful technology.

Now that we've looked at the types of AI, and touched upon its history, let's dive into how AI works.

## HOW AI WORKS

Depending on the specific type of tool, and the use case, AI can handle tasks that usually rely on some level of basic human intelligence. While AI systems can be complex, and there are a wide variety of types, the underlying principles of all AI rely on a few basic shared elements, steps, and processes:

- **Algorithms and models:** AI relies on mathematical algorithms and models to process and analyze the preprocessed data. An algorithm is a mathematical step-by-step guide that tells any AI model how to go about solving a particular problem. The model itself is a trainable computer program that scientists and users can interact with. The two are inherently linked, any AI model depends on an underlying algorithm.

- **Data collection:** AI systems start by gathering or being fed data from various sources. This data can be text, images, audio, or any other format, depending on the type of engine and specific model. The quality of the data used is of the utmost importance because AI learns and eventually makes decisions based on it.

- **Data preprocessing:** Raw data is often too noisy or unstructured for AI models to process and understand. Before these models can process some types of data, the data must go through a process of cleaning, and data-tagging, and then be transformed into a suitable format. This step also involves removing irrelevant information and redundancies, or dealing with missing or incomplete data sets.

- **Training:** ML and DL models need to be trained on labeled data. During training, the model learns to recognize patterns and make predictions. For instance, a machine learning model might train on a dataset of labeled images of various animal species to learn how to distinguish between them.

- **Feedback and Learning:** AI systems often receive feedback on the accuracy of their predictions, which helps them improve over time. This feedback loop is essential for reinforcement learning and other adaptive AI techniques.

These processes refine AI over time, allowing it to improve. Research, algorithms, and access to diverse datasets allow AI to learn new skills that will continue to make the tasks we carry out easier than ever. We're almost at the point where you can let your car drive you to your destination, so imagine how you'll be able to simplify your teaching load with the right AI tools!

### The AI Development and Training Process

Any AI model depends on a substantial amount of data, including text, images, and audio. These models are engineered, trained, and finely tuned to take input data and break it down into digestible snippets.

In natural language processing (NLP) tasks, like the ones often employed by LLMs, AI models attempt to approximate an understanding of what humans are saying, a process that includes making advanced contextual inferences.

This ability to model human understanding and inference-making processes is what ultimately allows them to gain what appears to users as a complex, nuanced understanding of language that makes it appear as if they have semantic acuity that approaches human levels.

The result of these carefully engineered and trained models is that the words they output take into consideration advanced elements such as tone and context from the words we use when engaging in chats with them.

Before any of these advanced tasks can be performed, AI engineers need to create a frame of reference for models to use in analyzing input data. This is achieved through the training process. *But how does it all work?* Here I'll explain the process in simple terms.

## AI Algorithms

Mathematics-based algorithms can be considered the foundational building blocks of the technology. As I mentioned before, algorithms act like a guide for AI models. What they do is provide computers with an actionable roadmap to work with data inputs, with the AI model and forward-facing software acting as the intermediary.

Algorithms enable AI models to learn from data and make smart choices that benefit human users. It's the algorithm that figures out patterns, makes predictions, or solves problems, depending on what the task required by the AI model requires of it.

To make any AI model work well and predictably, developers often need to try different approaches in creating a suitable algorithm to match the type of data processing tasks necessary. The next step involves the creation and training of the AI model that makes the powerful algorithm something that can be interfaced with.

## AI Training

A large part of the trial-and-error process inherent in any AI engineering undertaking involves the training of AI models. Think of what it's like trying to train a puppy. When training puppies, you show the dog what to do, and then give them a treat as a reward when they mimic the pattern you've asked them to replicate.

The dog eventually learns what behaviors get rewarded and becomes more predictable; its overall temperament and behavior are now linked to the behavior models you've successfully imprinted in its brain.

Like training a puppy, when you show an AI model examples, it learns to recognize patterns and make predictions. Unlike a puppy, however, most AI models don't operate off the type of reward-based and pleasure-seeking motivation systems that are unique to animals. There is one exception found in the case of a training technique called reinforcement learning. In this type of data training, the AI learns by getting rewards or punishments based on its behavior. Over time, it gets better at making choices to get more rewards.

There are a number of other ways to train AI that don't revert to this type of modeled punishment-reward system. In what's called supervised training, developers use a dataset where they already know the correct answers. It's like giving the AI a cheat sheet.

For example, if the model is learning to recognize objects in images, each image it receives will be tagged with a label telling the model the name of what's pictured. The AI model practices by comparing its guesses to these labels and adjusting to improve its own predictive accuracy.

In unsupervised learning, there are no cheat sheets. The AI has to figure everything out by itself. It looks at a bunch of data and tries to find hidden patterns or group similar things together. This can be useful for tasks like organizing data or making recommendations.

Transfer learning is another clever way that engineers teach AI models. It's like adopting a more mature, already well-trained dog, and then teaching it something new. In this case, you begin with an AI model that's already been through a training process, and then you fine-tune it for a specific task to save time and resources.

Training AI is a massive undertaking that relies on powerful computers, advanced graphics processor units (GPUs), and other types of dedicated AI chips. It can take a while, from hours to weeks, depending on how complex the model and the data are. The training process is a crucial step because it's what makes AI smart and able to make decisions without human oversight.

**AI Inferences**

After AI has gone through its learning phase, it can now apply its knowledge toward complex, real-world tasks, using inferences to analyze incoming data and generate predictive outputs that make sense.

For example, let's consider an AI model that's been trained on images of buses, and then it gets shown a picture of a car. It will likely infer that this four-wheeled vehicle appears to be some kind of micro-bus. While the model may not have the word "car" in its training data, it makes an inference that this is something similar to what it's been trained on.

This is how AI models, such as those used in computer vision (CV) tasks are able to recognize objects, making inferences from past data they were trained on, or processed previously.

The capacity of AI models to make logical inferences is what allows self-driving cars to drive safely, chatbots to talk with you, and medical AI to help doctors diagnose diseases.

## AI Feedback and Learning

AI systems learn and get better with constructive feedback, just like how people can learn from their mistakes. Feedback is crucial for AI, especially when it comes to reinforcement learning training techniques, as this input is what encourages the model to modify its behavior to achieve the reward it's been modeled to seek.

For AI that learns through unsupervised learning, the feedback process is a bit trickier. It takes more oversight to help the model discover the answers hidden in data.

AI models are often capable of checking their own answers against the right ones and addressing their own mistakes. This continuous process is repeated throughout training to improve the output, and in many instances, the model can continue learning once it's implemented and starts being utilized for real-life tasks.

In real-life use cases, like recommendation engines, it's your individualized user feedback, transmitted through your search history, consumption history, and metadata that matters most. This data about your personal activity is what allows AI to give you better, more accurate recommendations.

Feedback transmitted during the training process and once implemented is ultimately what makes AI useful, adaptable, and robust.

## AI Decision-Making

Some AI models have people's lives in their hands. Take autonomous vehicles for instance. Decisions like when to accelerate, how to steer around turns and avoid obstacles, and when to brake can make the difference between life and death. The overall intent of self-driving cars is to make roads safer, based on the premise that AI decision-making processes can actually perform better than error-prone humans in certain circumstances.

This belief has powerful implications. Aside from being able to drive us around town, AI can also tell us what might happen in the future based on past data. This predictive decision-making capacity has clear use cases in finance, where trading algorithms have already been implemented for some time. These buying and selling programs, unlike humans, make decisions without emotion, and without the fear that often characterizes market downturns or other times where volatility is present.

In the realm of health care, predictive AI decision-making technology has the potential to help flash the warning signs for disease outbreaks and make decisions around how to best contain them, again without the emotional fear-based elements that often inform human decision-making processes. These models can be great at spotting irregularities and have been implemented to prevent fraud and enhance security for financial institutions and their customers.

AI also has the potential to make things work better and to help address global problems such as climate change. From finding the fastest delivery routes to better managing resource allocation in a factory, AI-based decision-making can cut down on the carbon footprint of business activities by optimizing and streamlining processes and distribution networks. In the tech world, AI holds deep promise for data storage, cloud computing, and a wide range of custom-use hardware for IT, networking, or other systems architecture and infrastructure.

AI keeps getting smarter the more research in the field advances. The fact that it helps us make better choices, saves us time on repetitive tasks, and gives us intelligent ideas based on data, is why it can be such a beneficial tool for educators.

## AI MYTHS

Knowing how AI works and processes the data we feed it helps us better understand its capabilities. Despite all that it promises, there are still countless myths surrounding the technology. Some of these common misconceptions give us unrealistic expectations of what tangible benefits AI can offer us, while others point to ethical concerns and the technology's potential to be harnessed for nefarious, destructive purposes.

- **AI will replace human jobs.** While AI can automate certain tasks, it's unlikely to replace the need for human labor. Studies suggest that AI will change the nature of work by automating routine tasks performed by white-collar and administrative workers, allowing humans to focus on higher-value, creative, and complex tasks. A report from McKinsey & Company estimates that only about 5% of all occupations existing today have the potential to be fully automated (Manyika et al., 2017).

- **AI will make human expertise obsolete.** AI can complement human expertise but will never be able to replace it entirely. In fields like medicine, AI can assist in diagnosis and treatment recommendations, but the final decision rests with the healthcare professional.

- **AI can think and learn on its own.** AI models require continuous supervision, maintenance, and fine-tuning. They don't possess consciousness or self-awareness. Training AI models involves structured learning from data rather than the types of independent, creative thinking and learning capacities that humans possess.

- **AI can solve any problem instantly.** While this may be true with some complex mathematical computations, the problems we face as humans aren't all about number-crunching. AI's ability to solve problems we present to it is largely dependent on the specific AI model, the underlying algorithm, the task's complexity, and the quality of data it has been trained on and fed. Some AI tasks require substantial computing power and time for processing, making instant solutions unlikely for all problems.

- **AI is entirely objective and unbiased.** This of course can vary based on the specific learning model and purpose of the technology. AI models of all kinds can easily inherit, perpetuate, and magnify biases in the data used for training, leading to subjectivity in their output. Biased training data can lead to highly inaccurate, unreliable output. Understanding and addressing the biases that are inherent in almost any kind of AI model presents a whole range of ongoing ethical and legal challenges. Researchers and stakeholders throughout the industry are actively working to mitigate these inherent issues.

- **AI understands and reasons like humans.** While AI systems can mimic human-like patterns, they lack the general intelligence and reasoning abilities of humans. They operate based on patterns and statistical correlations in data rather than true comprehension as we understand it. AI can excel in specific tasks but doesn't possess common-sense reasoning or consciousness.

- **All AI technologies are highly advanced.** AI encompasses many different technologies, from simple rule-based systems to advanced deep learning models. Not all AI applications are equally advanced. The systems' capabilities depend on the specific technology and its level of development.

Being aware of these common myths around AI technology can help prevent the unwarranted fears and over-hyped expectations we see so often these days in the media and public sentiment. Recognizing the limitations and potential of AI is essential for responsible AI adoption.

AI technologies after all, like any technology, should ultimately serve to enhance human capabilities, giving us an extra boost to help us confront real-world problems effectively.

## Before We Move on

As we wrap up this chapter, we've demystified AI, moving beyond the buzzword to uncover its practical applications and the myths surrounding it. We've looked at how AI already permeates our daily lives, from voice assistants to smart devices, and we've explored its various forms, from machine learning to robotics. This foundational understanding paves the way for a deeper exploration of AI's role beyond our daily conveniences and into diverse industries.

Now it's time to start looking at how AI isn't just a tool for streamlining tasks, but can be seen as a transformative force that reshapes entire industries. In the next chapter, we'll be looking at how AI is revolutionizing sectors like healthcare, finance, manufacturing, and more, bringing innovations that were once the realm of science fiction into our present reality.

# 2

# THE ROLE OF AI IN VARIOUS INDUSTRIES

S ome people think of AI as something that's clearly innovative, but believe it to be a novel concept that can only be used in a few specific ways.

In my opinion, it's better to conceptualize it as a revolutionary, disruptive technology, like electricity! This may seem like a bold claim, but according to scientists at the forefront of the field, AI promises to make some fundamental changes and improvements to our day-to-day lives.

In the late 19th Century, electricity came into domestic spaces and allowed industrial manufacturing to expand its capacities without having to invest in new boilers, furnaces, and machinery to drive the wheels of their machines. Let's face it: Candlemakers and whale oil refineries were not happy at this time, but the convenience of being able to plug in and tap into local power grids fundamentally changed things for a society on the cusp of the modern era.

Similarly, AI is now transforming tasks in industries like healthcare, transportation, finance, e-commerce, and, of course, education, and it's up to us to spot which parts of the inefficient systems we rely on today might go the way of the Dodo. As educators, the influence of AI in education and in other fields is something we have to pay close attention to. The important thing to remember is that this technology isn't here to replace us, but to help us streamline our daily tasks and provide an overall better experience for our students.

Before we start discussing the use cases for AI in education in the chapters that follow, it's useful to take a closer look at how it's being applied in other fields. In this chapter, that's exactly what we'll be doing.

## AI IN HEALTHCARE

AI's emerging role in health care promises medical professionals a virtual medical assistant who never forgets a prescription, never misplaces a patient's records, and always knows how to pronounce words like "glucocorticosteroid" without stumbling. Whether or not they've taken the Hippocratic oath is unclear, but one thing's for sure: AI medical assistants deliver their advice in writing you can decipher!

One thing AI excels at is analyzing medical images like X-rays and scans. It can quickly and accurately spot troubling abnormalities, like the first signs of cancer, helping doctors and pathologists make accurate, often early diagnoses, and improving patient prognoses.

AI can also assist in screening for disease risk by looking at patient data, medical history, and genetics. It can even help predict transmission vectors, so we can act early to prevent outbreaks of disease.

As far as the treatment of diseases and medical conditions, AI is capable of analyzing a patient's data to suggest the best medicines and therapies. It helps doctors make better decisions by compiling and comparing patient info, up-to-date medical research, and current guidelines.

In the field of pharmaceutical research, AI models can analyze vast data banks of chemicals and substances, proposing new uses for existing drugs, and even assisting researchers in developing new drugs from scratch. This makes drug development faster and cheaper. AI also helps design better clinical trials to test new treatments.

AI can also be used for organizing, accessing, and analyzing various types of medical data, such as patient records and research. This helps researchers find patterns and discoveries that might be hard for humans to see. In the field of genetics, AI helps understand how genes relate to diseases and can help in generating personalized treatment plans based on this knowledge.

The applications of this technology in health care can improve the overall experience of patients, help doctors fine-tune diagnosis accuracy and detect diseases earlier, reduce mistakes, and make paperwork easier for doctors, nurses, and administrators.

In the healthcare field specifically, issues like data privacy and ethics concerns arise. When considering the incorporation of any kind of AI technology, whether it's in the classroom or the hospital, having people's sensitive, personal data in mind is of the utmost importance, making it important to disclose any use of AI to the people whose data is being utilized, and explaining in clear terms what their data is being used for.

## AI IN TRANSPORTATION

AI in transportation means you have a dependable road trip companion who never asks for snacks, doesn't need a coffee break, and never argues about the playlist. It can feel at times almost like you're driving with an old friend who has an innate sense of direction and never gets tired behind the wheel. An added plus is that this also comes without the backseat driving and annoying "are we there yet" questions.

AI-powered autonomous vehicles are at the forefront of today's transportation revolution. The technology promises to change how we get around, all while making transportation safer, smoother, and more efficient. Self-driving cars developed by companies like Tesla and Waymo use AI to drive, follow traffic laws, and avoid accidents (Lutkevich, 2023). These vehicles also help people who don't have cars or driver's licenses or aren't able to drive due to age or health reasons get where they need to go.

AI also could potentially help with traffic flow. In Los Angeles, AI-powered traffic management systems are already helping to optimize traffic light timings (Descant, 2021). These systems use real-time data from cameras and sensors to adjust signal patterns and respond to traffic flow. When sudden traffic jams occur, AI can provide data that tells traffic light programs to change the light durations in one particular direction to prevent backups.

Delivery companies like Amazon and FedEx are also using AI to make deliveries faster and cheaper. They're currently testing drones and self-driving trucks that use AI to find the best route, avoid obstacles, and drop off packages safely (Cain, 2022). As a result, delivery times and costs on certain items and types of deliveries can be reduced, leaving human workers to perform more complex delivery tasks rather than spending so much time navigating routes and dealing with traffic.

Seeing how AI has started to improve transportation, we can also start to gain a clearer picture of how the same concepts of optimization might apply to education. AI drones may not be able to replicate a teacher's skill set, but they can for instance assist in some interesting physics lessons for science teachers. Meanwhile, self-driving school buses could allow bus drivers to become more like aids or monitors, who are focused more on individual student needs rather than just getting them from point A to point B.

## AI IN FINANCE

Using AI in finance promises to empower investors, offering them a virtual financial advisor and access to advanced analysis tools. These digital brokers never sleep, they don't panic during market volatility, and won't complain about monitoring markets that are open 24 hours a day. It's like having a pocket-size Wall Street wizard without the expensive suits and fancy jargon about macroeconomics and key market indicators.

AI's applications in the finance industry are more than just about making things more efficient and performing autonomous tasks to free up more time for human workers. AI is already helping big brokerages and banks with risk analysis, stopping fraud, and giving better service to their customers.

Banks and investment firms, like many other businesses, have already begun to use AI chatbots to talk to customers. These bots can provide quick responses to customer queries, guide users through account management, and even assist with basic financial transactions. Bank of America, for instance, even has a chatbot named Erica that can give customers advice based on their spending habits (McNamee, 2022).

AI excels at identifying potential fraud. It's capable of looking at the patterns of how account holders spend money and can spot unusual activity. PayPal, for instance, uses AI to stop fake or potentially fraudulent payments, keeping customers' money safe (Sweet, 2023).

In equity markets, AI-powered algorithms are making light-ning-fast decisions. Some companies are starting to use AI to analyze market data and execute trades at speeds far beyond human capability. These algorithms aim to profit from minute market fluctuations. Some of these AI-fueled trading algo-rithms, such as Renaissance Technologies' Medallion Fund have already achieved significant gains in trading (Metz, 2016).

Lending institutions have started to employ AI for credit risk assessment. These advanced tools are able to look at loan applicants' financial history, employment data, and other factors to figure out whether they're a good fit for the lender. Peer-to-peer lending companies like LendingClub and Upstart have already started using this type of AI technology to offer more accurate loan approvals (Treece, 2023).

AI in finance isn't just about crunching numbers; it's making things better for customers, keeping money safe, and helping investors make smarter choices. Aside from their application in finance, the predictive algorithms used in the financial sector have the potential to revolutionize educational planning and risk assessment by offering data-rich analytical approaches that have the potential to enhance student success and overall educational outcomes.

## AI IN E-COMMERCE

The AI-powered tools being rolled out in today's e-commerce businesses are like having access to a personal shopper who knows your preferences even better than you do. Thankfully, unlike human shopping assistants, these virtual tools will never judge any questionable fashion choices you make! AI helps you more easily window shop in your pajamas without having to schlep down to retail outlets or interact with any overly enthusiastic salespeople who are competing with their coworkers over sales commissions.

AI has already been rolled out in the industry, where it's enhancing customer experiences and business operations. One notable way it does this is through AI-driven recommendation engines. These tools analyze how customers behave, what they've bought, and what they look at online. The algorithm then suggests products tailored to customers, helping businesses sell more and making the shopping experience smoother and more enjoyable for the consumer.

Visual search tools are another area in which these advanced tools are improving. Instead of wasting time trying different search terms or scrolling through products, shoppers are now able to upload an image of what they want. Products that are either identical or very similar get pushed to the customer based on the visual input, making the shopping experience streamlined and satisfying.

AI-driven algorithms have also improved inventory management, buying, and planning. They can look at past sales and factors like the weather and holidays to predict what products will be in demand. This helps businesses avoid overstocking and running out of products, or holding too much inventory. It also gives retailers further flexibility to adjust prices based on demand, competition, and historical data. This type of fluid pricing strategy helps e-commerce companies maximize their earnings and stay competitive year-round.

AI doesn't stop there in the world of the online shopping experience. It personalizes your experience even before you visit a retailer's website. AI tailors website content, emails, and ads to match your personal preferences. It's like having a store that's curated just for you! The ads and promotions you receive show up when and where they should, helping you find things you need—*and* things you didn't know you needed!

AI-powered chatbots are also ubiquitous in today's world of online shopping. These chatbots provide real-time customer support by answering questions and helping you choose products. Their 24/7 availability aims to make sure that customers have a positive experience while shopping online even if they have questions when customer service centers are closed.

## INTRO TO AI'S ROLE IN EDUCATION

Now that we've seen how AI is already working its magic in healthcare, transportation, finance, and e-commerce, it's time to explore its potential applications in education.

For students, AI grants instant access to the world's most patient 24/7 tutor, one who can explain the Pythagorean theorem or mitochondrial function. For teachers using AI in education, there are a number of exciting potential uses. Here, I'll run through the major ones.

- **Individualized learning and data:** Imagine being able to analyze student data with ease, helping us customize educational content and strategies for each individual learner. AI represents a promising potential solution to the age-old question of how to boost learning outcomes while sparking classroom engagement. It allows timely interventions for struggling students and paves the way for improved teaching methods.

- **Accessibility and inclusivity:** AI can increase engagement with students who require extra attention, or who already rely on adaptive technology. It offers ways to better incorporate the needs of students with various learning challenges into classroom dynamics. Boasting both speech recognition and text-to-speech capabilities, AI holds promise in assisting students with learning and intellectual disabilities, ensuring they can participate in all types of educational activities.
- **Productivity and efficiency:** AI can be your trusty teacher's assistant, taking care of tedious administrative tasks, giving you more time to focus on creating engaging content and materials, planning lessons, and addressing students' individual needs.
- **Adaptive assessments:** Let's face it: Test scores and grade scaling systems can be highly flawed, and fail to show an accurate representation of your classroom's and individual students' overall progress and their grasp of course material. AI-powered exams can dynamically adjust to each student's ability level and learning style in real time, providing precise measurements of their skills and progress. It means more accurate evaluations and valuable feedback.
- **Research and content creation:** Another excellent use for AI that's particularly effective for educators and researchers is that it can give them quick access to information that they don't have expertise in, but that may be adjacent to their field or course material being prepared. While it's not good practice to rely on AI for research, it can be a quick, creative way to get the juices

flowing. Moreover, it can save you time, allowing you to dedicate more to the core focus of your research, and conceptualizing how to put it into effective classroom content.

- **Professional development:** Whether you work in academia or grade-school level, AI can act as a secondary voice aside from the colleagues and mentors you already depend on for ideas and feedback. From studying your teaching methods to suggesting tweaks to curricula you developed based on student performance, the instant feedback loop offered by AI can empower you to refine your teaching techniques.

- **Scalability:** Through integration into some online courses and platforms, AI has the potential to open up educational offerings to a broader audience. From translation into other languages to administrative assistance with managing enrollment numbers that far exceed what one professor can manage, the possibilities are vast. Just look at how massive open online courses (MOOCs) and remote learning skyrocketed during the COVID-19 pandemic (Impey & Formanek, 2021). AI promises to provide tools that can help make MOOCs and other remote learning opportunities feel like a more intimate classroom environment, offering everything from personalized guidance to virtual TAs with a solid knowledge of the course material.

Speaking of Covid times, the pandemic truly was a turning point for AI in education. As students embraced remote learning, educators found themselves on platforms like Zoom for the first time, faced with the difficult task of translating in-person lessons into the virtual realm.

In the midst of this profound transformation, a remarkable study at the college level explored the power of AI-driven grading tools (Rutner & Scott, 2022). The goal was to see if AI could assess the quality and relevance of student posts in online discussion forums. The results were impressive. AI-powered grading was largely successful in automating the assessment of student discussions. Moreover, the AI's evaluations closely matched those of human graders.

But, as with any emerging technology, there remains a substantial amount of doubt around the incorporation of this new technology. The same study sounded a cautionary note, reminding us that we must continuously refine AI models to capture the subtleties of in-person student interactions. In essence, what this case study reveals is the immense potential of AI in education, serving as a glimpse into a future where grading becomes streamlined and time efficient.

It's also a poignant reminder that the technology needs further refinement and rigorous training and testing standards to ensure that this type of tool can navigate the intricacies of student interactions in any kind of remote, online, or hybrid setting.

### Before We Move on

We've now seen the diverse landscapes where AI is making significant strides, from healthcare to transportation, and from finance to e-commerce. Each example illustrates AI's transformative power, showcasing how it can bring efficiency, precision, and innovation to various sectors. But more importantly, these examples pave the way for understanding the potential of this powerful technology in education.

In the next chapter, we'll see how these insights gleaned from other industries can help us address the unique hurdles in the educational realm. The next chapter is all about the complexities and nuances of integrating AI in educational settings. In it, we'll take a look at the challenges educators face, from ethical considerations and data privacy to adapting teaching methods and curriculum design. This exploration will help us better understand how to take advantage of AI's potential responsibly and effectively in the classroom, ensuring that it becomes a tool for enhancement rather than a source of complication.

# PART II

## WHY DO EDUCATORS NEED AI?

# 3

# CHALLENGES EDUCATORS FACE

Teaching is a bit like trying to herd cats. With classrooms brimming with unique personalities, sometimes they all decide to go in different directions.

Every day, teachers all across the world aim to meet their classrooms with patience and a sense of humor, in addition to handling all their other responsibilities and obligations. This is where AI comes in, promising to support educators, empowering us to approach the classroom environment with more energy and more attention to our students' individual needs than ever before.

The truth is that, in the ever-evolving landscape of education, we sometimes can feel like we're on one of those spinning playground rides, and about to fall off! *Do you ever feel like you're on an endless spinout? Have you grappled with challenges that seem to have no clear end or resolution sight?* If you have, you're not alone. The demands of today's classrooms extend far beyond the traditional roles of an educator, posing a wide variety of complex peripheral concerns to deal with, including understanding and addressing diverse learning needs, technology integration, and the pursuit of improved student outcomes.

School administrators *can* offer more support, but in many cases, these promises end up becoming nothing more than hot air. Like us, their hands are tied as they struggle to meet state and federal guidelines. By leaving teachers to tackle whatever comes up in the classroom, today's public school systems expect us to perform multiple jobs at once, which can easily lead to burnout.

As we start looking at the pillars and pitfalls of modern education in this chapter, a clearer picture emerges, showing us that AI really can be a game-changer. Rapid technological advancements and shifting pedagogical paradigms can make us all feel like we're losing traction and falling behind, but I guarantee you that once you discover the transformative power of AI and how it promises to redefine the future of learning, your worries will start to recede.

## PERSONALIZATION

In today's modern educational landscape, there's no one-size-fits-all approach. Teachers are charged with the difficult task of teaching toward various differences, such as language, cognitive abilities, prior knowledge, and family backgrounds. The old idea of teaching the same way to everyone just doesn't work in the kinds of dynamic educational settings we find ourselves in.

Meeting the needs of a diverse group of students is a complex and stressful undertaking. Educators have tried various methods and resources to meet the needs of individual students, aiming to personalize education; however, these methods often fall short due to factors and limitations beyond our control. This is where the opportunity to incorporate AI presents itself. Here, I'll show you what it can offer:

- **Differentiated instruction:** Whether it's preparing tiered materials for different reading levels or working on special homework for students on the autism spectrum, AI can help with tasks related to the creation of differentiated learning materials.
- **Learning Management Systems (LMS):** Digital platforms and LMS are used frequently to share information and assignments. While some of these systems offer customized learning modules, they might not always adjust quickly enough to meet each student's ever-changing needs. AI-powered LMS technologies promise to streamline these platforms, dynamically shifting content and the manner in which it's presented based on classroom data and metrics.
- **Formative assessment:** Formative assessments monitor students' progress and help us tweak our teaching accordingly. These assessments are helpful but often provide insights after the fact. Early intervention through AI-powered insights may help us gain these insights earlier, allowing us to address problems and patterns before they're revealed through more traditional modes of assessment.

- **Learning analytics:** More and more, data-driven approaches are being employed in education. The thing is, to effectively incorporate data into pedagogy, teachers often need help in understanding how to apply the data. Data alone may not give a detailed picture of each student's strengths and weaknesses or their unique learning preferences. This is where the power of AI algorithms comes in, as they promise to improve the quality of the insights we can glean from data, and give actionable recommendations based around them.
- **Teacher collaboration:** Many schools encourage teachers to work together and share information about their students to better tailor their learning experiences. While this is a good human-focused approach, it relies on having enough time and resources for such collaboration, which can be limited. AI promises to help with this by incorporating teacher insights together into reports that can fuel dialogues between teachers, and help them make sure students' needs are addressed across different subject matters.
- **Technology-assisted personalization:** Certain educational tech tools claim to offer personalized learning by adjusting content and speed based on a student's performance. However, these tools can be expensive, and their effectiveness can vary. AI can improve and fine-tune these types of tools, making them more accurate and useful.

Current approaches have limitations because they often struggle to meet the needs of each student. It's tough to find the time and ability to adapt and provide truly personalized learning experiences. AI comes in as a potential solution to fill this gap. AI can handle a lot of data, adjust in real time, and offer personalized content and support.

One example of this type of lapse that could be aided by AI is the way that students with dyslexia often find it challenging to learn to read in traditional classroom environments. They're liable to become frustrated and lose focus when they don't have access to personalized solutions like one-on-one help, or specialized reading programs. However, schools that offer personalized reading support for dyslexic students could see significant improvements in reading skills and increased engagement.

Likewise, language learning can be tough in diverse classroom environments with students from various linguistic backgrounds and varying levels of command of the English language. When teachers use standardized language instruction without considering each student's level of language proficiency and cultural context, students may lose interest. On the other hand, personalized language training with specific support for each student, which can be bolstered through the use of AI, could lead to better learning outcomes and increased engagement.

As educators grapple with the complexities of meeting diverse student needs using current methods and tools, the limitations of these approaches become more evident. Achieving true personalization remains challenging due to practical constraints and the ever-changing nature of individual learning paths. However, the promise of AI is on the horizon, offering the potential to overcome these limitations in a variety of novel use cases.

AI, with its data-driven insights, adaptability, and scalability, promises to provide educators with more effective and immediate options for personalization. By harnessing the power of these advanced tools, educators can free up their hands while gaining insights that aid them in navigating the complex landscape of diverse student needs.

## TECH SKILLS

The promise of enhanced learning experiences, instant access to a vast array of information, and the ability to adapt to individual student needs has ignited a fire of enthusiasm for the integration of AI technology in education.

There are, however, a number of distinct challenges that loom like a shadow over classrooms on the brink of AI integration. Some of you out there may even find yourselves in a state of tech trepidation. Let's face it: The rapid pace at which technology evolves can leave even the most dedicated educators feeling like strangers in a digital land.

It's not a lack of passion or commitment; it's simply a matter of keeping up with the relentless advancements. We all know the fear of accidentally clicking the wrong button, the dread of losing precious work, or the anxiety of not knowing how to troubleshoot a technical glitch, all of which can be paralyzing.

But, here's the silver lining: Every educator who steps into this digital frontier is on a transformative journey. We're delving into unexplored territory, on a path to learn, adapt, and eventually master these digital tools that promise to empower the next generation with the tools they'll need to thrive in an ever-changing world.

The gap between technology and teachers may seem daunting, but every click, every mistake, and every "aha" moment brings us closer to harnessing the full power of technology in education. AI tools designed with user-friendliness in mind can serve as motivation for us to pick them up and start learning! These tools can serve as our digital allies, bridging the gap between teaching as we know it today and the advanced tech that makes Silicon Valley tick.

The bottom line is that these tools really can offer a helping hand, making the integration of advanced technology into education more seamless.

By making technology more accessible, and less intimidating, user-friendly AI tools really can empower us educators to take advantage of this technology.

That's why in the chapters that follow, we'll focus on exploring the AI tools that can help us transition from tech novices to confident users, unlocking a plethora of opportunities for innovative and effective teaching. In this way, AI represents not just a solution to a problem but rather joins us in a cooperative effort toward redefining education. It promises to make the journey of technology integration smoother and more rewarding for educators and students alike.

## DATA ISSUES

In education, over the last decade or so, data has started to play a fundamental role, serving as a way star that's able to provide actionable guidance to teachers, administrators, and policy-makers. The incorporation of this type of data and analytics in our education systems promises to enhance the learning experience and ensure student success.

Educators need to understand how well their students are doing, what areas they're excelling at, and what areas they might need extra help in. The kind of comprehensive understanding afforded by data and analytics helps create a more personalized learning experience for each student, ensuring nobody gets left behind.

Moreover, data empowers educators to track improvements over time. By comparing current data with past performance, teachers can see if their students are making progress. It's like checking a fitness tracker to see if you're getting healthier. This allows educators to see the impact of their teaching methods and interventions, making classroom instruction more effective.

Another crucial aspect is early intervention. Data helps identify students who might be struggling, allowing educators to provide extra support by catching a minor issue before it becomes a big problem. With early warning systems fueled by data and analytics, schools can ensure students get the help they need to succeed.

Data also helps when it comes to accountability and equal access to education. It shows how well schools are doing and helps them demonstrate their commitment to achievement. Being able to quickly crunch and compare data related to standardized test scores or other performance metrics can help schools assess whether they're delivering a good education.

Furthermore, data is a vital tool for making continuous improvements to education. The field is constantly changing, and data helps teachers and schools adapt. By making informed adjustments based on data, educators can provide a better education that meets the evolving needs of students. It promises that school systems set clear educational goals, allocate resources wisely, and focus their efforts on achieving them. With data, education stays relevant and effective in a rapidly changing world.

Many educational apps and platforms already rely on user data to create personalized gamified student experiences. Popular learning apps, such as Duolingo, can dynamically adapt to a student's progress, making learning more engaging and enjoyable. As with these popular apps, gamification in educational software used within schools allows students to earn rewards, badges, or points based on their achievements, and the data collected helps teachers track their performance.

Adaptive learning software collects data on students' responses to questions and assignments. It then adjusts the difficulty of the questions in real time to match each student's skill level. It's almost like having a personalized tutor that tailors the learning experience to the individual. Games like "Kahoot!" and

"Quizlet" allow students to compete and have fun while learning. These platforms collect data on each student's answers and provide feedback. Teachers can use this data to identify areas where students need more help.

These fun, engaging examples showcase how data is being harnessed to make learning more personalized. Data isn't just about school metrics, and tracking student progress—it's about making improvements, intervening early, ensuring accountability, driving continuous development, and informing smart planning. It represents a promising way in which we can create a more holistic educational landscape.

### Challenges Teachers Face

Manually collecting and analyzing data in education can be difficult for teachers. Firstly, there's a lot of raw data to deal with, and secondly, managing it effectively can be a challenge in itself. This can lead to mistakes, or the inability to glean any useful insights from all the data.

Manual data collection takes a lot of time. Spending too much time collecting and assessing data can detract from the big picture problems, causing tunnel vision. Another problem is accuracy. Humans aren't infallible, and the ways in which they piece together data can often be biased or incomplete, making information collected manually less reliable than automated data.

Performing data analysis tasks manually can be repetitive and tedious. To do so effectively, teachers need the right tools to make sense of all the data they've collected, which can limit their ability to use it effectively for teaching.

## The Importance of Data Privacy

Another challenge confronted by teachers in data collection is data privacy. This issue comes into play with manual collection methods, and also when AI has access to vast quantities of student data.

When teachers handle sensitive student data manually, rather than this information residing in secure databases, there's a higher risk of information getting into the wrong hands or getting lost, which could potentially be a big problem. Leaving things up to AI software tools, and the tech companies that engineer them also represents a potential data privacy problem, especially when it comes to public institutional use of these proprietary tools.

These factors and data privacy concerns underscore the importance of school systems designing their own robust data privacy protections, and in some cases relying on building their own proprietary AI tools over utilizing commercially available ones. Relying on private companies to store and process students' information could in some cases go against the ethical standards public institutions are bound by, so in the case of public school systems, the issue has to be considered wisely.

The mishandling of student data can have serious repercussions. The extensive collection and utilization of data in today's educational settings raises concerns over how this information is stored, accessed, and protected. Mishandling sensitive data can lead to privacy breaches and expose students to various risks, including identity theft and unauthorized sharing of personal information. The misuse of student data can erode trust in educational institutions, both public and private, as parents and students may become wary of sharing their information or engaging with digital learning tools due to privacy concerns.

AI may come to play a controversial role in education when it comes to data. While it can assist in data analysis, schools and educators must be committed to making sure these new tools maintain data privacy standards. As mentioned before, certain types of AI models can assist in safeguarding data. They're capable of monitoring data access, detecting unauthorized breaches, and enhancing overall data security, warning administrators of potential data breaches.

A crucial factor to look at when assessing the viability of any use of AI within educational institutions is what level of access the company that builds the software in question does with their data, and what level of access they'll have about your users. AI's ability to harness the power of data for educational enhancement is promising, but this has to be coupled with an effort to maintain high data privacy standards. This way, AI in our schools can contribute to a safer, more efficient, and more effective educational environment where student data remains protected, and the learning experience continually evolves to meet individual needs.

## LIMITED RESOURCES

Passionate educators too often face challenges that compromise their ability to provide top-notch learning experiences. Among these hurdles, resource constraints are some of the most common. Manifesting in various guises, these challenges—be it limited time, the quest for suitable educational materials, or the elusive presence of classroom support—tend to bind teachers up in a knot.

Amid this picture of pedagogical constraints faced by teachers today, a glimpse of hope emerges—the infusion of technology and the potential that AI represents. These innovative tools hold the promise of lightening the load and amplifying the educational journey for both teachers and students alike.

Teachers in the United States spend an average of seven hours each week buried under a load of burdensome administrative tasks (Hardison, 2022). This includes the relentless job of grading, juggling lesson plans, and handling data entry. These are precious hours that could be better spent in the classroom, interacting with students and imparting knowledge.

A recent study by the Brookings Institute reveals that only a meager 12% of public school teachers in the United States have the luxury of a full-time classroom aide or assistant (Ladd et al., 2021). This means the majority of teachers find themselves navigating the unique needs of their students without any backup support.

These statistics highlight the daunting challenges that educators face daily: demanding student-to-teacher ratios, an overwhelming time commitment to administrative tasks, a scarcity of educational materials, and an alarming shortage of class-room support. Faced with these resource constraints, teachers who are committed to maintaining quality standards must explore innovative solutions. This is the way to ensure that the efforts we put into education lead to tangible results and remain accessible to all students.

Resource constraints aren't just hurdles for educators, as they tend to affect students' learning trajectories and outcomes, too. These limiting factors too often place the burden on teachers, making it harder for them to provide top-quality instruction. This, in turn, can limit students' access to high-quality educational materials and individualized support. It's a challenge that impacts teachers and students alike, and finding solutions to these constraints is essential to creating a more effective and equitable educational environment.

By taking on time-consuming administrative chores like grading and data entry, AI promises to unshackle teachers from the clutches of mundane tasks and the challenges presented by resource constraints, allowing them to dedicate more time to the heart of their profession: teaching. With the assistance of AI, educational materials can find their way to students in more efficient ways, and personalized support becomes a reality. It promises to support educators in creating learning environments that are both productive and profoundly engaging.

INTRO TO HOW AI CAN HELP

Machine learning algorithms in particular are capable of shouldering the weight of time-consuming administrative responsibilities, from grading assignments to data entry. AI-driven systems overall can help us efficiently manage and distribute resources. Another key ability of these tools is their ability to adapt to new data dynamically, bridging resource gaps and promoting educational equity among diverse student bodies.

AI-driven grading systems, like Turnitin and Gradescope, have already helped teachers trim down their workloads. These tools can efficiently assess and provide feedback on student assignments. Learning management systems (LMS) such as Blackboard, Canvas, and Moodle have begun to incorporate AI elements aimed toward helping educators personalize learning pathways for students. Relying on AI algorithms, these new tools can recommend content, assignments, and resources to teachers based on individual student progress and needs.

Adaptive learning platforms such as DreamBox, Knewton, and Smart Sparrow also use AI to adjust content and pacing based on student performance, ensuring that each student receives instruction tailored to their skill level and learning pace (Baraishuk, 2023). These AI tools empower educators to be more effective and responsive in their teaching, ultimately benefiting students by providing tailored instruction and support.

Amid all these new technologies emerges the exciting potential that these tools could in fact fundamentally reshape the way we teach and learn. The fusion of AI and education holds the promise of a more efficient, personalized, and equitable learning experience for all. The landscape continues to evolve, and educators and students alike are poised to reap the benefits of this intelligent partnership for decades to come. But before the next steps are taken, the grounds for these changes must first be laid.

## SHIFTING TO ACCOMMODATE A WORLD WITH AI

As educators, today we find ourselves at the crossroads of a significant transformation. This shift is bound to be one that carries profound implications, underscoring the importance of understanding the capabilities, as well as the problems, posed by AI.

If there's one thing that's undeniable, it's that this pivotal force will continue to weigh heavily on the way students learn and prepare for their future. We must not merely observe this transformation as it occurs but need to actively adapt to harness its full potential while addressing the challenges head-on. As educational technology evolves, it's important to note that this doesn't give us a mandate to step back and take less responsibility—rather, we educators need to assert our role as a guiding force that empowers students to navigate an AI-driven world responsibly.

The job market is evolving, with AI literacy emerging as an indispensable skill. To keep students competitive in the work-force of tomorrow, educators will play a pivotal role in imparting AI-related knowledge. We must prepare our students to thrive in an AI-dominated landscape, ensuring they are future-ready.

The presence of AI in education presents an exciting set of opportunities. Educators need to be at the forefront of this transformation, and that's why our adaptability will be key to shaping the future of learning. Embracing AI benefits students, and helps ensure that we don't allow the tech companies that design these systems to make decisions for our students.

The first exhilarating leap into this new world for many of us will be through the world of professional development. Teachers of all subject matters and levels should eagerly seek opportunities to level up their AI know-how through workshops, online courses, and dynamic collaborations with fellow educators already riding the AI wave.

The next step is integrating the potential of these AI tools into our teaching toolbox. Whether it's starting with smart assessment tools or introducing adaptive learning platforms, each of these small steps can end up revolutionizing the way we craft and deliver lessons.

Collaboration is the secret sauce of this exciting journey. Educators need to form dynamic alliances and cross-disciplinary communication and sharing platforms to empower colleagues with their own AI experiences, challenges, and triumphs. This collaborative spirit fuels the development of AI best practices, and can lead to the development of collaborative, innovative teaching techniques. This is ultimately how we'll be able to stay on the cutting edge of this educational revolution in the face of great change.

Fostering a growth mindset is key to the coming reframing of the educational landscape. Embracing change and adaptability is the name of the game here, and this attitude is the way that we can unlock the full potential of AI. It's partially about embracing the thrill of the unknown, but ultimately about brushing up on our own skills while future-proofing our careers. With this growth-oriented mindset, we can effectively lead our students into an AI-driven future.

### Before We Move on

As we move into the next chapter, we do so with the newly ingrained understanding that AI isn't just about reducing our workload. It's about transforming how we teach and how our students learn. In the next chapter, we'll delve deeper into our exploration of AI-driven personalized learning, looking at how these technologies can tailor education to individual student needs, interests, and abilities.

As you'll begin to see, today we stand at the threshold of a new era in education, where AI's capacity to customize learning experiences promises to unlock each student's full potential. It's an exciting journey from the conventional to the cutting edge, where AI's capacity for personalization promises to reshape the educational landscape.

# 4

# THE POWER OF PERSONALIZED LEARNING

## WHAT IS PERSONALIZED LEARNING?

In short, this refers to instruction that's tailored to individual students' needs. It's widely known as one of the most effective ways of teaching today, but of course comes with steep requirements on the teacher's part in terms of both planning and flexibility.

With so many demands on our time already as educators, it's easy to let these more personalized forms of instruction slip through the cracks in favor of our tried-and-true methods. This is especially true in public school settings where concerns over meeting strict state and local school board requirements often take precedence over trying out new pedagogical approaches.

Personalized learning moves away from standardized lessons with the one-size-fits-all mentality many school systems and institutions adopt out of either convenience or necessity. The personalized approach empowers students to learn at their own pace, spending more time in troubled areas or immersing themselves in subjects that interest them. This way, students are able to quickly make their way through work they can easily grasp without needing to wait for others to catch up.

To achieve personalized learning, teachers will often modify their strategies and materials to suit a diverse range of learning styles. Using digital tools and resources, like AI-powered adaptive learning technology, can simplify this process. This way, one master lesson plan can be used to create several individualized variant options.

## WHY CUSTOMIZING LESSONS FOR EACH STUDENT MATTERS

Customizing lessons for each student used to be a major time drain, but even before these AI tools began to emerge, it was effective in making a difference, especially for learners with learning disabilities, sensory issues, or other challenges. For these students, teachers can use individualized education plans (IEPs) and 504 plans as the basis for the lesson planning that's crafted to help these students succeed. This type of learning can empower students and make them feel confidently in control of their education instead of lost in the process.

Now that we have a number of fast, convenient ways to approach making customized lesson plans and course materials at our disposal, there's really no excuse not to give it a try.

Any student, even those without disabilities or other special needs, processes and learns information in ways they understand. When they can relate to the subject matter, and the way in which it's delivered, they engage more with the material. Some visual learners, for example, may prefer to see information presented in charts and graphs, while others prefer to listen to the presentation. Some students don't learn until they try something on their own and then get feedback from the teacher, which again requires more time and effort on the educator's behalf.

Another thing we often have to deal with is what students already know, or don't know. In many cases, especially in primary-level education settings, students often lack some foundational knowledge that puts them at a disadvantage when you teach new concepts. It's like they're trying to complete a puzzle while missing half the pieces.

AI tools can address these basic knowledge gaps in young learners by tailoring questions based on their responses to general polls and surveys conducted in the classroom or can be introduced dynamically in the case of learning apps. Let's say, for example, a fourth-grader is starting an online math assessment and aces the first few questions. The program will then start giving harder problems. When the student struggles to answer those, the algorithm adjusts the questions to help the student practice the concepts they haven't yet mastered.

## CHALLENGES AND CRITICISMS OF PERSONALIZED LEARNING

While personalized learning presents a promising approach to education, it is essential to recognize that, like any educational paradigm, it is not without its challenges and criticisms. Acknowledging these aspects is crucial for a comprehensive understanding of the overall landscape.

One prominent challenge to incorporating these methods further into education today revolves around data privacy. With the integration of AI and personalized learning technologies, there is an increased reliance on collecting and analyzing vast amounts of student data. This raises concerns about how this sensitive information is handled, stored, and protected. Ensuring robust safeguards to preserve the rights of students becomes imperative in the face of evolving technologies.

Despite the clear benefits of personalized learning, there remains a risk that its implementation could in some ways exacerbate existing educational inequalities. Access to technology and resources varies among schools and communities, and not all students may have equal opportunities to benefit from personalized learning initiatives. This makes it even more crucial to address these disparities to prevent the creation or perpetuation of educational divides.

Striking the right balance between personalized learning and standardized assessments poses a considerable challenge. Education systems often rely on standardized tests to evaluate student progress and teacher effectiveness. Aligning personalized learning approaches with these types of rigid metrics that are still widely relied upon is an ongoing challenge.

Another potential barrier toward further incorporating personalized learning comes in the form of vocal resistance from educators, parents, or policymakers who may be skeptical of its efficacy. Addressing misconceptions and providing evidence of positive outcomes are essential steps in overcoming this challenge and fostering a supportive environment for innovation in education.

What becomes evident is that personalized learning requires a number of steps to be taken to ensure that parents, school administrators, and teachers are aligned over the approaches and that they also meet local, state, and federal standards. AI presents unique opportunities in personal learning, as it can both exacerbate and mitigate some of these challenges already by educators incorporating personalized teaching methods.

## HOW AI TOOLS CAN ASSIST

While AI poses its own challenges, it can also act as a powerful ally, providing a vast array of tools specifically designed for educational personalization. These tools aim to enhance the learning experience by tailoring content to individual needs.

### Personalized Learning Platforms

These platforms are designed to cater to the unique needs of individual students, offering a dynamic and adaptive learning experience. The technology is based on adaptive learning algorithms. These algorithms continuously assess students' performance, understanding their strengths and weaknesses. By analyzing data on how students engage with content, the platform is able to adapt in real time, tailoring the educational journey to each individual student.

One of the most valuable features of these types of platforms is their ability to deliver content tailored to each student's proficiency level. Whether a student requires additional support in a specific concept or is ready to advance to more challenging material, the platform adjusts the current learning level and trajectory curve accordingly.

What these types of platforms offer teachers is comprehensive progress monitoring and instant feedback, giving them insights into individual student performance and identifying areas of improvement. Likewise, students can expect to receive more timely feedback, helping them foster a more involved, metrics-based approach to their learning that isn't based on how they compare to others in their class.

In this way, personalized learning platforms can help promote a greater sense of autonomy among students. By tailoring the educational experience to individual preferences and pacing, these platforms encourage self-directed learning. Students can delve deeper into topics of interest or seek additional support where needed.

This versatile functionality that focuses on learning differences represents a vast opportunity that can be applied to assisting students with learning challenges of various types and degrees. To accommodate these diverse learning styles, personalized learning platforms offer a variety of resources. From visual aids and interactive simulations to audio components, these platforms ensure that content is presented in a way that's tailored to fit each student's preferred learning modality.

The data teachers and schools can receive from these types of platforms go way beyond traditional assessments like standardized test scores. The platform aggregates data on students' interactions, learning preferences, and progress. This information empowers teachers to make informed decisions, refining their instructional strategies to better suit the needs of their specific classroom.

The interactive element that many of these types of platforms can offer is another advantage worth mentioning, as many of them include features that allow for real-time collaboration and support. Students can engage with peers outside of school hours on course materials and subject matter, can share insights with each other, and can remotely collaborate on homework assignments.

With all this talk about these platforms, you're likely curious to know what some of the top personalized learning platforms being used today are. Here's a list:

**General Usage Personalized Learning Platforms**

- **To Teach:** A versatile, personalized learning platform designed to empower educators by helping them generate lesson plans and course materials through a user-friendly interface. For more information, check out their website: https://to-teach.ai/

- **Tutor AI:** Uses AI to offer personalized tutoring services to both teachers and students on any subject matter they may not be well-versed in. You can learn more here: https://tutorai.me/
- **PeerAI:** This tech learning tool integrates collaborative learning into personalized education. It employs AI to facilitate peer interactions, quizzes, and study groups, encouraging knowledge-sharing and collaborative problem-solving among students. If it sounds interesting to you, you can learn more here: https://peerai.org/
- **Adaptiv Academy:** Specializes in adaptive learning solutions for educators. It provides tools to create personalized online courses, helping students master concepts through tailored instructional content powered by AI. To learn more, visit: https://app.adaptiv.me/app/
- **MyLessonPal:** A comprehensive platform that assists educators in designing personalized lessons based on vetted, evidence-based content. It incorporates AI to drive engagement with students, helping concepts get driven home. For more information, visit their website at: https://mylessonpal.com/
- **CourseMind:** A management tool that helps online education platforms and other groups organize courses, and get their messages out to the public around course offerings. Teachers may find it useful in the planning of extracurricular school activities, or as a resource for developing online courses outside of their in-school

instruction. To learn more, visit: https://coursemind.io/

- **Coursable.io:** Provides students with study guides based on vetted, fact-based sources from across the internet, allowing them to develop personalized guided self-study courses. For more information, check them out at: https://coursable.io/
- **MAGMA Tutor:** Another AI tutor that personalizes content based on the user, helping them achieve their learning objectives. To learn more, visit: https://magmatutor.com/

**Subject-Specific Personalized Learning Platforms**

- **Chat2Course:** Uses a conversational AI tutor to enhance the learning experience specifically in subject matter pertaining to health and wellness. It provides interactive features, including ones that allow the platform to be used for human-to-human collaboration. For more details, visit: https://chat2course.com/
- **JustLearn:** Allows students to don the appearance of customizable 3D characters as they interact with human and virtual language tutors from all across the world. If it's something that sounds fun to you, your students are bound to love it too. Check out their website at: https://www.justlearn.com/

**Personalized Learning Platforms For Young Learners**

- **eSpark:** Specializes in K-5 education, delivering personalized lessons on reading and arithmetic that are aligned with curriculum standards. The platform utilizes AI to identify learning gaps and provide targeted resources to support student growth.

*Integration into Preexisting Teaching Methods*

One of the notable strengths of these AI-powered personalized learning platforms lies in their adaptability, and their ability to complement existing teaching methodologies. Rather than necessitating a radical departure from established practices, these platforms can enhance traditional teaching methods and help with student engagement.

One way to use these tools is to start integrating the platforms into their lesson plans to reinforce key concepts or provide additional practice opportunities for learners who need a bit of extra help outside of class time.

The flexibility afforded by these useful platforms, and the fact that many of them are designed to use only vetted, curriculum-friendly, fact-based information allows for seamless alignment with existing educational standards. Teachers who administer these platforms can direct the platform's content to the curriculum's learning objectives and content requirements.

The best part of all these tools is that far from threatening our jobs, they're designed to make them easier. When we choose to incorporate them into our instruction, we're also able to maintain better control over the customization of learning paths. While the platform offers adaptive features, the fact that it allows teachers to curate specific learning trajectories based on their understanding of students' needs is an added plus. This customization ensures that the platform aligns with the pedagogical goals of the entire classroom.

As we discussed previously, the integration of real-time data into teaching practices is a hallmark of these learning platforms. Through them, we can receive insights into individual student progress, allowing for targeted interventions. This targeted approach enhances the precision of overall instructional strategies, enabling timely and effective support and responses from administrators based on teacher feedback.

Another asset that's useful to us educators is that these platforms are perfect for remote or blended learning environments. Whether in a traditional classroom or a virtual setting, with classes composed of present or remote students, or a mix, we can incorporate these platforms to create a blended approach that works for all cases. This flexibility accommodates a number of different situations, including ones like we experienced during the pandemic.

The integration of AI-driven tools in educational institutions opens avenues for professional development among educators. Training initiatives, sponsored by schools and school districts, can familiarize teachers with the functionalities of personalized learning platforms, empowering them to harness the full potential of these new tools.

From the ever-important perspective of parents, the incorporation of these learning platforms shows a commitment to a student-centric approach within the classroom. As educators get more comfortable with using these platforms effectively, students can become more active participants in shaping their own educational journey. This shift toward student agency contributes to a more engaging and participatory overall learning environment.

The ever-important feedback loop between educators and students can be strengthened through the integration of personalized learning platforms. Educators can provide targeted feedback based on real-time data, while students receive immediate insights into their progress. This iterative feedback loop promotes continuous improvement.

### *Looking at Real-World Applications and Case Studies*

While personal learning is a promising way for schools to improve student prospects and educational standards, there are several challenges when it comes to actually integrating these types of programs. The first challenge is often in convincing parents that the kind of tech-world adjacent basis for incorporating new technologies is grounded in studies and research that confirm the efficacy of such systems.

Failed objectives such as the "one laptop per child" program, a nonprofit in the mid-aughts that attempted to address the problems faced by students in the developing world by putting technology in their hands, highlight the need for more than just giving every kid a Chromebook. A 2019 New Yorker article called "The Messy Reality of Personalized Learning" provides us with a valuable case study with which we can start to glean some information on the incorporation of personalized learning into public school systems, in this case, a grant-receiving school in a small rural Rhode Island town called Issac Paine Elementary School.

The grant received from the state of Rhode Island's Office of Innovation allowed Issac Paine to join the state's "lighthouse school" pilot program, an initiative designed to bring tech into schools, allowing teachers and administrators to work on blended curricula that mixed traditional pedagogical methodologies with laptop-based learning through apps and gamified study tools. The program itself was a joint initiative between the state and tech companies brought in by then-state Commissioner of Education Deborah Gist, who happens to be from a family of Silicon Valley philanthropists.

At the core of this "lighthouse school" program at Issac Paine is the student-first approach that comes with this technological integration. The students are allowed to progress at their own pace, and the flexibility afforded by the blended instruction methods accommodates learning differences, allowing for individualized progress. From interactive projection screens that display syllabi and charts, to math exercises that take place online on the Chromebooks, these tools keep the students engaged while they're learning.

As suggested by the title of the article, with any of these new ways of learning, there are bound to be challenges and growing pains—in the case of personalized learning initiatives, frequent screen time concerns, privacy issues, and in some cases an increase in teacher workload. Equally important is looking at the financial backing behind such initiatives, as they're often financed by tech mavens who have a vested interest in shaping American public education in their image, blurring the lines between the interest of private enterprise and public institutions.

What is clear is that with any of these types of programs, the need for teacher training is paramount. Luckily, for us educators, there are several different programs around the country that are training teachers specifically for these changes, including New England Basecamp and Highlander Institute, which are both nonprofit organizations dedicated to this type of upskilling.

Another key insight gleaned from the lighthouse initiative in Rhode Island is that periodic assessment and reevaluation of the program's efficacy will be key. By incorporating the feedback of educators, students, and parents, personalized learning methods can be fine-tuned, hopefully mitigating the challenges and concerns that frequently pop up around them in their early phases, smoothing out all the bumps in the road as they're identified.

### Addressing the Double-Edged Sword Posed by AI in Education

While AI in the classroom offers a wide range of benefits, we also have to be upfront about the fact that it can lead to increased opportunities for student plagiarism and cheating. As AI-powered tools are further integrated into classrooms already relying heavily on tech-based personalized learning, new ethical standards and means of assessment must be paired with them.

Aside from tools being employed in the classroom, the ease of access today's students have to advanced LLM chat tools, such as ChatGPT and Google's Bard, create further challenges when it comes to assessing written homework assignments. Students can easily write entire essays about subjects they have no knowledge of at the click of a button, without the need for any research on their part.

Just like math exams that require students to show their work, making sure that they aren't relying on calculators to solve simple division equations, for example, new standards need to be introduced in student-written assignments to ensure that their work doesn't become overly reliant on these powerful tools, which can be helpful to students when used correctly.

### Strategies for Responsible AI Use

While an entire book could be written on this subject matter alone, there are a few key areas we can look at when it comes to crafting responsible use policies for AI in our classrooms. Here are a few starting points:

### Ethical Guidelines and Policies

Develop clear and comprehensive ethical guidelines and policies governing the use of AI tools in educational settings. These guidelines should emphasize the importance of academic integrity, responsible technology use, and consequences for violating established norms.

- **Awareness campaigns:** Students need to know about the ethical implications of using AI tools. Empower them with the knowledge to discern between legitimate use for learning enhancement and unethical practices such as plagiarism or cheating.
- **Push for greater transparency in algorithms:** Educational institutions and teachers should collaborate with AI developers and the tech companies that supply them with personalized learning products, rather than following the lead of non-educators when it comes to how these powerful tools make decisions.
- **Stay vigilant:** Regularly review any AI-generated content used in teaching materials you prepare, or in any assignments you're grading. Intervene promptly if academic dishonesty is identified in student work.
- **Promote AI literacy:** Integrate AI literacy into your classroom curriculum, providing students with an understanding of how AI works, its capabilities, and what your ground rules are.
- **Participate in professional development:** Take advantage of any development opportunities offered to learn the latest developments in AI and its applications in education.
- **Community engagement:** Engage with various members of your school community, including students, parents, and fellow educators, to create a

collective understanding of the responsible use of AI in education.

- **Continuous evaluation of AI technologies:** Regularly evaluate the impact of any AI tools you've introduced to your classroom and be willing to adopt strategies based on feedback from administrators and peers, as well as your own insights and observations.

*Before We Move on*

Personalized learning, enhanced by AI, represents a pivotal shift in our approach to targeted education. As we've seen, AI's ability to customize learning experiences caters to the unique needs and pace of each student, fostering a more inclusive, effective, and engaging educational environment. However, this journey is not without its own set of challenges and ethical quandaries.

As was made evident in the case study we looked at, in some ways personalized learning initiatives can make even more work for us teachers. That's why in the next chapter, we'll be shifting our focus to the well-being of educators. Teacher burnout is an increasingly pressing issue, exacerbated by the multifaceted demands of modern teaching, including AI integration. Here, we explore how, rather than representing a daunting challenge, AI can serve as a support system, offering practical solutions to alleviate some of the burdens we carry.

# 5

# CUTTING DOWN BURNOUT AND SAVING TIME

B urnout isn't a sign of weakness; rather, in some ways, it can be seen as a cry for greater efficiency. In the demanding world of education, where we teachers balance the needs of students with administrative burdens and the constant pursuit of pedagogical excellence, burnout has become an all-too-common reality. This chapter confronts the stark reality of teacher exhaustion, a phenomenon marked not just by fatigue, but by a profound sense of being too often overwhelmed and underappreciated.

Burnout is more than a mere occupational hazard, it's actually a barrier to providing effective instruction. It manifests not only in emotional strain and physical tiredness but also often in a diminishing passion for teaching—a profession in which we all know energy levels and enthusiasm must be maintained in order to thrive.

In the environments we work in, with high demands and too often limited resources to draw from, AI can offer us some practical assistance. Automating mundane tasks is a great way that we can enhance our work-life balance, but that's just the beginning of what these advanced tools offer us.

## WHAT IS BURNOUT?

Teacher burnout, a term increasingly heard throughout the halls of educational institutions worldwide, encapsulates a state of emotional, mental, and often physical exhaustion caused by prolonged stress and frustration. It's not just about feeling tired —burnout is a more profound sense of disillusionment that can easily erode our passion for teaching.

In essence, burnout is the teacher's response to the chronic stress of the educational environment itself. It manifests through symptoms like emotional fatigue, where we might feel drained and unable to muster enthusiasm for our work. Physical symptoms are also common, ranging from headaches and sleep disturbances to more serious health issues caused by prolonged stress.

Statistics paint a stark picture of this crisis. According to a study, in the U.S., 44% of K-12 teachers reported feeling burned out "often or always," while for professors of higher education, these figures stand at a still-elevated 35% (Bouchrika, 2022). As the numbers reveal, this phenomenon isn't isolated to any one region or type of school. Instead, it's a widespread issue that's affecting educators at all levels.

The roots of teacher burnout can be difficult to ascertain. What we do know is that we educators often find ourselves swamped with administrative duties that can be both time-consuming and repetitive. The pressure to meet curriculum standards, coupled with the challenge of addressing the diverse needs of students, can create a perfect storm of stress.

Emotional strain also arises from managing classroom dynamics and sometimes dealing with a lack of support or understanding from parents and administrators. Teachers at the K-12 level are expected to be child psychologists and social workers in many cases as well, explaining the higher reported rates of teacher burnout at those grade levels.

Planning lessons, grading assignments, and managing class-room activities—tasks that are integral to teaching—can become sources of immense pressure when we're already overexerting ourselves in other areas. Our desire to provide quality education often means taking work home, leading to blurred boundaries between professional and personal life for many of us.

So, you might be wondering: *What can AI do to help with teacher burnout?* Let's explore.

## AI TOOLS FOR TEACHER BURNOUT

Today we have access to a variety of tools that are not only enhancing the learning experience for students but also promise to significantly alleviate the workload for educators. These AI tools are specifically designed to address various aspects of teacher burnout, offering solutions that range from administrative task automation to personalized student support. Let's explore some of these innovative tools, and take a closer look at exactly what kinds of assistance they can offer us.

### Grading and Peer-to-Peer Assessment

AI-driven assessment ed-tech platforms, including popular ones like Gradescope and Turnitin are revolutionizing the grading process. Gradescope is capable of assessing student assignments, quizzes, and exams. It can provide instant feedback to students, significantly reducing the time teachers spend on grading.

Turnitin is geared toward upholding academic integrity, and its plagiarism-detection tools are frequently relied upon by teachers and academic institutions. But that's not all they offer. They also have several tools available for generating feedback on written work and on grading and assessment.

Teachers have reported that these tools have transformed their assessment processes, freeing up hours each week that can be dedicated to other tasks. There are also some AI tools making waves for their innovative approaches to what's known as peer-to-peer assessment.

Platforms such as PeerGrade facilitate this type of learning and assessment, fostering a collaborative learning environment. Teachers using these platforms have observed improved student engagement and reduced pressure on themselves to be the sole source of feedback, allowing students to critique and grade each other's work.

### Lesson Planning

Lesson planning tools, including personalized learning platforms like Athena by EduPhoria, and instruction planning tools like IBM's Watson Education Teacher Advisor, use AI to provide teachers with personalized lesson planning tools.

Teacher Advisor is geared specifically toward grades K-8, while Athena covers all grade levels and can even be used in professional training contexts, and for teacher professional development, focusing on adaptive learning paths for all levels.

These types of integrated platforms offer a wealth of resources and strategies tailored both toward meeting individual class needs and curriculum standards, significantly reducing planning time. Educators using these tools have noted a marked decrease in their planning workload, enabling them to focus more on in-class engagement.

### Administration

Collaborative list-making and project management tools that have integrated AI components, such as Trello, are helping teachers manage their schedules, reminders, and administrative tasks more efficiently. They're also great for faculty-wide initiatives, including curriculum planning, the planning of extracurricular activities and after-school programs, and coordinating fundraising activities.

These types of tools can automate email responses, schedule appointments, and help with classroom management, reducing the administrative burden on teachers and facilitating communication between colleagues and administrators.

*Analytics*

AI tools like BrightBytes and GoGuardian offer data analysis capabilities, providing teachers with actionable insights into student performance and behavior based on data.

BrightBytes calls itself the "leading fully managed data and analytics platform for education." As you might imagine, it works by collecting large amounts of data and then putting it into visualizations that facilitate data-based decision-making. The goal is to improve academic trajectories, while also improving the overall well-being of students, hopefully relieving teachers of some of the burden often felt by them.

These types of tools might seem complicated, but they can really help in identifying areas where students need support, enabling targeted interventions without the exhaustive manual analysis and guesswork previously required. There are, however, some distinct ethical challenges that arise with these tools.

GoGuardian is one such case, as it's essentially a digital surveillance tool that allows teachers to spy on students' social media accounts. The stated purpose of these tools is to monitor students for potential signs of violence; however, the ramifications of such tools represent a difficult area, as they could lead to unfair targeting and profiling. That said, they're geared toward student safety, which is an ever-important concern in America, particularly as school shootings continue to plague school systems across the country.

## *Tutoring*

For students who need extra help in specific subject matters, there are a number of subject-specific AI tutors that can help, alleviating the burden on educators who provide extra help through labs or after-school tutoring sessions. One such tool is Hypatia, a step-by-step math tutoring program that helps students learn in a natural, intuitive way.

Like many of the personalized learning tools we've already looked at, Hypatia makes customized assignments based on individual progress and level of competency.

## *Teacher Testimonials*

An important aspect of assessing these tools, and thinking about the ways we might integrate them in our own classrooms, is looking at how others have successfully applied them. A great place to turn in looking for this type of advice is Reddit, and in one particular thread entitled "What is the most creative way to use AI in the classroom?" we're able to glean some key insights. Here are the key insights and takeaways:

## History Comes Alive

Reddit user FreeHat0690 highlights the use of AI as a virtual tutor and for simulating conversations with historical figures. This creative application has been beneficial in engaging students in a more interactive and personalized learning experience. The same user also mentions the use of AI in providing feedback on written work, which has eased the burden of grading and allowed for more efficient classroom management.

## Boring Tasks Made Easy

Another aspect where AI shines is in handling the grunt work of drafting emails, creating syllabi, and brainstorming project ideas. This was pointed out by the same Reddit user, FreeHat0690, who recommends ChatGPT for its user-friendly interface and reliable outputs. This tool has enabled teachers to focus more on pedagogical planning and student interaction, rather than getting bogged down by repetitive administrative tasks.

## Creating More Fun, Engaging Learning Experiences

User kiran-verma45 shares an imaginative application of AI in creating customized and interactive learning experiences. By using AI-generated characters and immersive virtual environments, educators can enhance engagement, empathy, and comprehension among students. This approach not only fosters creativity and critical thinking but also reduces the stress of developing engaging content from scratch.

**Efficiency in Mathematical Problem Creation**

Alpinecardinal, a math teacher, shared their experience of using AI to create math problems. While they prefer not to rely on AI for lesson notes, the tool has proven useful for tutoring and generating new problems, thereby saving time and effort.

**AI in Managing Workflows**

Virtu1931, another Reddit user, notes that tools like Magicschool.AI have been effective in making workflows more efficient for teachers. This kind of AI application helps streamline various teaching processes, thereby reducing the workload and stress for educators.

These testimonials from real educators demonstrate the significant impact AI tools have in reducing teacher burnout. From automating administrative tasks to creating engaging learning experiences, AI is proving to be a valuable ally in the fight against the pressures of modern teaching. As we continue to explore AI's capabilities, it's evident that these tools can not only improve the efficiency of teaching but also contribute significantly to the well-being and job satisfaction of educators.

(*What Is the Most Creative Way to Use AI in the Classroom?*, 2023)

## CHALLENGES AND RISKS OF USING AI TO COMBAT BURNOUT

Integrating AI into the educational landscape, while promising to alleviate teacher burnout, brings with it a distinct set of challenges and risks that require some careful consideration. One of the primary worries is the potential for overreliance on technology. As educators increasingly lean on AI for various tasks, there's a risk of a growing dependency, which could lead to a knowledge gap in traditional teaching skills and methodologies. This dependence is further complicated in situations where technology might fail, leaving teachers feeling unprepared and reliant on tools they no longer have at their disposal.

Alongside the issue of overreliance, data privacy of both the teacher and their students poses a significant concern. AI's effectiveness in education often hinges on its ability to process and learn from large volumes of student data. This raises questions about the security and privacy of sensitive information related to students' learning patterns and personal details, while teachers may also be exposed to these data privacy risks depending on what kind of information they share about themselves. The ethical handling and protection of this data is paramount to maintaining trust and integrity within the overall educational ecosystem, guaranteeing a safe future for the data of teachers and students alike.

Another challenge that arises with the introduction of AI tools in education is the feeling of tech fatigue, particularly for educators who are older, or who simply aren't as technically adept. The rapid integration of new and evolving AI technologies can lead to drastic increases in stress for some teachers, ironically contributing to the burnout these very tools aim to reduce in the first place. The learning curve associated with these technologies can be quite steep, and the pressure to keep up with the latest advancements can add an additional layer of stress to an already taxing profession.

To navigate these challenges effectively, today's educators are charged with a complex multi-forked mandate. We need to adopt a balanced approach to technology integration, while also paying special sensitivity to our own teaching preferences and our own technological aptitudes. One key concept I'd really like to stress is that we should be using AI as a supplement to traditional teaching methods rather than a complete replacement. The balance between AI tools and time-tested pedagogical methods is ultimately what will help ensure that we retain and refine our core teaching skills while benefiting from the efficiency and support these new AI tools offer.

Like introducing any new academic subject matter or teaching method, acclimating your classroom to AI tools in education should be a gradual and continuous process. Educators should make a concerted effort to engage in ongoing professional development and stay abreast of the latest developments in AI, while seeking to understand its ethical implications in the field. Starting with one or two AI tools and gaining complete proficiency in them before introducing more can help manage the feelings of trepidation around feeling constant pressure to adapt to the newest and most powerful technologies.

Creating a supportive environment for students and your colleagues is key to successful AI implementation. This includes things like making sure they have access to technical support, sharing best practices among colleagues, and fostering open discussions in your school about the challenges and benefits of rolling out AI systems in your classroom. Regular meetings and the solicitation of feedback on the effectiveness of AI tools are crucial. This approach allows educators to make informed adjustments based on their own experiences, and those of colleagues, ensuring that AI tools effectively reduce the overall workload while also enhancing the level of instruction, rather than simply adding to the complexity of the acts of lesson planning and instruction.

By carefully considering and addressing the inherent challenges posed by AI, educators can harness the full potential of AI in reducing burnout, ensuring that it serves as an effective tool in enhancing their professional lives, rather than a source of additional stress.

### *Before We Move on*

The emergence of AI tools in the educational landscape represents a promising avenue for many of us in the fight against teacher burnout. These tools offer practical solutions to some of the most pressing challenges we as educators face today, from reducing the burden of administrative tasks to enabling more personalized learning experiences for students. It goes without saying, but of course, the integration of any type of AI into teaching practices must be approached with a sense of balance, care, and consideration for the privacy of our data and that of our students.

The promise of AI in education lies not just in its advanced technological capacities, but in its potential to rekindle the passion for teaching within all of us, by alleviating some of the common burdens that lead to burnout. As we move forward, it remains imperative that we harness these tools thoughtfully, ensuring they serve to enhance the teaching experience rather than complicate it, or hinder the progress and development of our students.

Now that we've taken a look at how AI can ease teacher burnout, while still stressing the importance of using these tools responsibly, our exploration into what these advanced tools offer us takes us to the next crucial step. In the upcoming chapter, we'll jump into the exciting ways that we can utilize AI in education that are safe, smart, and beneficial for everyone involved.

# HELP OTHER TEACHERS TRANSFORM THEIR CLASSES INTO OASES OF PERSONALIZED LEARNING

*"Some people call this artificial intelligence, but the reality is this technology will enhance us. So instead of artificial intelligence, I think we'll augment our intelligence."*

— GINNI ROMETTY

In the Introduction, I mentioned that millions of teachers are already embracing AI in their classrooms to keep up with the latest technological advances, streamline their lesson planning, and personalize their classes. The ease with which AI can be used to create customized content for different students is helping them promote an authentic love of learning and strike the right chord with every single student.

You have seen that there are a myriad of apps and tools that complement existing teaching methodologies and blend seamlessly with existing curricula. AI is flexible, affordable, and fact-based, making it a best friend, guide, and handy time-saver for current-day educators. If what you've read so far has illuminated new possibilities for AI in your classroom, then I hope you can spread the word.

**By leaving a review of this book on Amazon, you'll show teachers how to manage their time and customize their classes according to each student's needs.**

By letting other educators know how AI tools and techniques can complement rather than replace their talents, you'll free up their time for what truly matters—connecting with their students and igniting a passion for knowledge.

Thank you so much for your support. Together, we can help our students appreciate how enjoyable learning can be.

**Scan the QR code below**

# PART III

## HOW TO IMPLEMENT AI

# 6

# SAFE AND SMART: DATA-DRIVEN DECISIONS

"Data is the new oil, but ethics is the new compass" (*Clive Humby*, 2021). As British mathematician and entrepreneur Clive Humby so aptly put it, the essence of our current technological era is characterized by a quest toward rectifying the ethical oversights of the past.

In the world of education, where data proliferates every aspect of teaching and learning, this statement carries a weighty poignancy. In this chapter, we'll be exploring the power of data-driven decision-making in education, a facet of this new technology that's worth exploring more deeply. *Why?* you might ask. Well, as we navigate today's data-rich landscape, the ethical use of AI becomes that much more apparent and important.

This chapter is solely dedicated to equipping you with the knowledge and tools to utilize AI in making informed, data-driven decisions without breaching any social or ethical lines that might compromise the efficacy of the data at our ready disposal. We'll be taking a closer look at the finer points of handling sensitive student data, the ethical implications of AI in education, and the overarching legal frameworks that govern its responsible use in educational institutions.

## HANDLING STUDENT DATA WISELY

Student data can be considered a digital asset that we can use to shape effective and responsive teaching methodologies. It tells us vital information and statistics about each student's learning journey, preferences, challenges, and successes. Consequently, the handling of this data demands not only precision but also a profound sense of responsibility and care.

With this insightful data comes a whole new set of risks and obligations for educators. The management of this sensitive data itself is laden with risks. Privacy breaches stand as one of the primary concerns, posing a threat to the confidentiality and security of sensitive student information. The repercussions of data breaches are not just limited to legal consequences, as they can also erode the trust between students, parents, and educational institutions. The misuse of sensitive student data, whether intentional or accidental, can lead to misinformed decisions that adversely affect a student's educational experience and progress, potentially further perpetuating bias or inequality already present.

Best practices for data handling involve a combination of technological savvy, ethical consideration, and a deep-rooted commitment to overall student welfare and outcomes. It's a responsibility that extends way beyond the rules set by administrators and school boards, as it also becomes about an acknowledgment of gaining "insider" knowledge that has the potential to profoundly shape a student's educational journey. As educators navigate this tricky terrain, the need for a measured, informed, and ethical approach to the handling of this sensitive data emerges as a moral imperative.

## THE ETHICAL USE OF AI

As AI systems increasingly exert an influence in educational settings, their ethical implications come to the forefront. AI's role in the near future will extend from executing simple administrative tasks to shaping institution-wide pedagogical approaches, making its ethical use a necessity to uphold the integrity of teaching and learning in the years and decades to come.

The data in question, when it comes to ethics concerns, can range from academic performance metrics to personal and behavioral information. The handling of such sensitive data raises significant privacy concerns. There is a constant risk of data breaches, which could lead to the unauthorized access and sharing of personal information, potentially causing harm to students and eroding trust in the educational institutions that hold their data.

Another crucial ethical aspect to be aware of is fairness. AI algorithms themselves, if not designed and monitored correctly, can inadvertently perpetuate and amplify biases. This could spell unequal treatment for students based on racial, class-based, or other demographic attributes. Such biases in AI decision-making can have long-term detrimental effects on student outcomes, perpetuating inequality and injustice throughout the educational system.

The ethical use of AI in education also takes into account the impact that AI-driven decisions may have on students. AI's involvement in areas like grading, personalized learning, and behavioral assessment means that decisions outsourced to a machine can significantly affect a student's educational experience, sometimes with minimal intervention on the teacher's behalf. It's crucial to ensure that these types of decisions are executed in a way that's fair, transparent, and conducive to student growth.

In order to start navigating these ethical considerations, it's useful to look at some guidelines and recommendations for the ethical use of AI in educational settings:

- **Upholding transparency and accountability**: Ensure that the workings of any AI systems being used in your classroom are transparent. Educators and students alike should understand how the AI tools you're utilizing make decisions, and there should be accountability mechanisms in place for AI-driven results, such as grades.
- **The importance of inclusivity in AI design processes:** Involve diverse parties in the design and implementation of custom-built AI solutions. This inclusivity can help mitigate biases and ensure the AI systems being used in your school cater to a broad spectrum of student needs that fit with the

demographic composition and diversity of your student body.

- **Practicing regular audits and updating systems:** Regularly audit AI systems for any biases or ethical lapses and update them accordingly. Continuous monitoring ensures that AI systems evolve and adapt to ethical standards and educational needs that match the needs and special considerations of your student body.
- **Define student data privacy rules:** Implement clearly laid out data privacy protocols. Only collect data that's necessary, and ensure that it's stored and processed securely, respecting privacy and confidentiality.
- **Promote ethical training and awareness:** Educate colleagues and students about the ethical aspects and inherent biases of AI. Training should cover both the potential benefits and the ethical pitfalls of AI's applications in education.

## HOW TO UTILIZE AI IN SAFEGUARDING AND GATHERING STUDENT DATA THE ETHICAL WAY

The secure collection and storage of student data is one of the primary concerns in today's educational settings, as the systems and services they offer become increasingly reliant on insights gleaned from databases that contain sensitive information about the student body. With the addition of AI to this already increasingly data-reliant landscape, questions of ethics are bound to arise.

While this reliance on powerful technology for processing and analyzing students has its own distinct set of concerns associated with it, these same systems can in fact enhance privacy and security. In this way, today's advanced AI tools, applied in institutional settings, can help gather and store data safely, while also protecting it from potential breaches or misuse.

Recent technological advancements have made available new types of systems for securely collecting and storing student data. Tools like cloud-based storage solutions offer encrypted and secure platforms where educational data can be stored with a high level of security. These systems often come with advanced features such as access controls, audit logs, and regular security updates, ensuring that student data remains protected against unauthorized access.

According to a study by the Global Security Operations Center, AI cybersecurity tools can protect data from being compromised faster, and at a lesser cost than traditional cybersecurity tools (Lehmann & Durfee, 2023). The data points to the efficacy of new, advanced tools such as IBM's Security QRadar Suite, and how they can save institutions money.

While both public and private institutions tend to be structured differently than businesses, it's worth looking at cybersecurity threats for their potential drain on finances. According to IBM, data breaches cost companies an average of $4.35 million per incident in 2022 (Arampatzis, 2023).

You might be wondering how this all works. To put it simply, AI algorithms excel at monitoring and analyzing patterns in data access and usage, enabling them to detect anomalies that might indicate a potential breach.

Aside from these types of warning systems, they can also assist in automating authorization processes, ensuring that only those with the proper credentials and certificates have access to specific sets of data. Through advanced encryption and fire-walls, they offer fortress-like protection. This is particularly important to prevent fraud and extortion and can help secure data in publicly funded institutional settings where data privacy is not just a technical issue, but a legal one as well.

## LEGAL ASPECTS OF DATA AND AI

To ensure full legal compliance, administrators and educators must meet a complex set of legal requirements and standards, ensuring that their use of AI and data management aligns with local and federal laws.

Though it can vary by geographic region, several legal frame-works govern the use of AI and the handling of data in educational settings. These laws and standards are designed to protect the privacy and rights of students and to ensure that the data is used ethically and responsibly.

Laws, including the Family Educational Rights and Privacy Act (FERPA) in the U.S., dictate how educational institutions can handle personally identifiable information from student records. There are also international standards, such as the General Data Protection Regulation (GDPR) in the European

Union, which provide guidelines on data protection and privacy.

In addition to these, there are specific legal considerations when it comes to the use of generative AI. Most of the lawsuits around AI issues have in fact been focused around generative technologies like LLMs. Training data, when sourced in ways that breach copyright law, can become subject to legal action.

Though students' proprietary works and creations aren't necessarily points of concern in this area, especially at K-12 levels, educators should be aware of the fact that certain AI systems will be using and, in some instances, retaining parts of student work, including original work which *could* be subject to copyright law.

This could include student-created works of fiction, poetry, art, or other creative endeavors shared with or processed by in-school AI systems, but could also extend in some cases to essays, book reports, and a plethora of other common homework assignments.

## BEST PRACTICES FOR DATA-DRIVEN DECISIONS

In order to utilize student data in ethically and legally sound decision-making processes, educators should adhere to a set of best practices that ensure the safe and effective use of data and AI tools. This makes sure that the principles outlined in the No Child Left Behind Act are upheld, and that data like poor test scores and lapses in classroom comprehension are used in ways that increase the prospects for better learning, rather than penalize or create unfair standards or assessment metrics that end up making the problem worse.

Our observational capacities and our ability to glean useful, actionable insights from data are often determined by our adherence to a specific set of standards and best practices. Here, I'll explain:

**Be mindful of potential bias.** By committing to an unbiased analysis of data, educators and administrators can gain valuable insights, some of which may be unexpected or previously unknown. The elimination of bias from student data not only supports the validation of existing beliefs but also opens up avenues for new perspectives and discoveries.

**Be clear about defining your strategy.** By identifying and articulating specific goals, such as determining the most effective programs for closing achievement gaps or aiming to improve math scores on state tests by a certain percentage, educators can narrow their focus to specific tasks. This approach enables us to concentrate our efforts and resources on achieving these well-defined objectives, leading to more targeted and effective outcomes.

**Focus on relevant, actionable data and straightforward lines of inquiry.** The types of questions to consider might include examining student and teacher performance, chronic absenteeism and its impact on academic success, or the effectiveness of intervention strategies. Given the vast amount of data available through various sources like student information systems, learning management systems, and other assessment tools, it's important to pinpoint and collect only the relevant data needed to address the specific issues being targeted. This approach ensures that the data collection process is focused and efficient, leading to more effective problem-solving.

**Have clearly defined targets and goals.** It's crucial to define solid metrics for what exactly constitutes progress and then set benchmarks at various levels. Depending on the level you're implementing these changes on, this could mean district-wide changes, localized metrics on each campus of an institute that has satellite locations, specific standards in each classroom of a school, or simply guidelines that are set for individual teachers and students.

**Closely follow any problems that may emerge.** Closely follow and promptly address any problems that may emerge during the implementation of strategies or in the course of achieving set targets. This proactive approach ensures that issues are identified and resolved quickly, preventing them from escalating and negatively impacting the educational process. By staying alert and responsive to emerging challenges, we can maintain the effectiveness and integrity of the strategies we roll out, ensuring they align with our goals and objectives.

**Create regular reports.** Accessible reporting is key to this process, as it ensures that the data and its implications are clear and understandable to all involved. Sometimes reports can lead to more questions than answers, creating a cycle of requests that can be time-consuming and frustrating, especially for teachers who are already managing tight schedules. To avoid this, it's suggested that data be made easily accessible, not just to staff and administration but also to teachers, students, and the wider community, helping fuel greater levels of engagement and participation. (McKean, 2022)

### *Before We Move On*

Now, armed with the knowledge of how to navigate the data-driven landscape safely and ethically, it's time to turn our attention to the practical applications of AI in education. In the next chapter, we'll look at how AI can streamline any teacher's daily routine, making it easier and more efficient. From reducing workload to enhancing the overall teaching experience, there are numerous ways just waiting to be explored!

# 7

# STREAMLINING EVERYDAY TASKS

There are several different ways AI can help us streamline our daily tasks, reducing our workload and supporting us in enhancing the overall teaching experience, for ourselves, and for our students. From automating administrative tasks to providing personalized learning experiences for students, AI isn't just a practical tool but is also a dynamic partner in the educational process. In this chapter, we'll look at some real-world examples and innovative approaches where AI has successfully transformed the traditional tasks of educators, making their day-to-day activities more efficient and impactful.

## AUTOMATING ADMINISTRATIVE WORK

Let's face it: We too often find ourselves inundated with administrative tasks that, while necessary, can significantly consume our valuable time. These tasks range from grading assignments and marking attendance to creating schedules and lesson plans.

Each of these activities, essential as they are, can detract from the time and energy we can otherwise invest in direct student engagement and innovative teaching methods.

Grading is a time-consuming task that requires both attention to detail and fairness. Marking attendance daily is another routine yet essential task, ensuring accurate records of student participation. Preparing exams involves not just question creation but also ensuring they align with learning objectives and educational standards. On top of this, creating syllabi and class schedules are both complex tasks that require balancing multiple factors, such as classroom availability, student needs, and curriculum coverage.

AI's potential uses in reducing some of the burden of these common tasks present us with a revolutionary approach to handling some of the less exciting aspects of what we do. After all, the primary goal of educators is to educate, *right?* Let's take a look at some of the ways these tools can help in the areas mentioned above:

**Grading:** Today's AI tools, such as TurnitIn, which we mentioned previously, are being used to grade a wide range of assignments in various subjects. Depending on the institution and country, manual grading procedures often involve active review from two teachers, with the final grade being a composite based on the average of the two scores given (Kumar, 2020). This especially applies in cases where the assessment criteria and subject matter are more open, and it's not simply a matter of right or wrong answers, such as with grading written work. Today's paper-grading AI tools are capable of reading and assessing a wide range of topics, in all types of formats, from essays to straightforward multiple-choice exams. They're also able to deliver prompt and useful feedback, which can then be supplemented by the reviewing teacher's additional comments.

**Exam preparation:** Teachers of all levels have felt a substantial amount of pressure to incorporate AI into their classroom policies and directives. For some, this means placing restrictions on the use of AI, and for others, it means embracing these changes by educating students about acceptable use policies, and permitting them to use it in specific ways. For some, this has extended to test preparation, and some teachers have chosen to actively encourage students to use AI chatbots to prepare for exams by using them to administer practice quizzes. In a poll conducted by Education Week, 40% of teachers reported that they'd integrated discussion about or use of AI into their classroom instruction in some way (Prothero, 2023). Even for teachers who remain wary over the use of AI in their classrooms due to the potential for plagiarism, it's important to recognize how AI, particularly chat-based LLMs, can be extremely useful to students when applied in this way, especially when looked at next to more traditional methods for exam preparation such as manually written flash cards.

**Attendance:** While the ethics of facial recognition machine learning algorithms are a subject that warrants its own discussion, numerous governments, such as China, have been rolling out these types of systems on a wide scale for some time now. Whether or not the implications of these types of tracking tools are appropriate for use in our Western education systems is up for debate. What is clear is, whether through facial recognition, or through other, perhaps less invasive methods, such as the use of IoT (Internet of Things) devices, automating attendance-taking can relieve teachers of some of this burden, and let them get straight to teaching, rather than waste time with worrying about roll call.

**Syllabi:** AI, particularly LLMs, represents a promising way for teachers to rapidly craft syllabi, or at least the basic starting points for them, without expending too much mental energy. The ability of chat-based LLMs to structure and organize data allows for a speedier process that allows teachers to spend less time formatting their syllabus document and more time honing the course content and the overall structure of the course topics and class material.

**Scheduling and planning:** AI-powered tools, such as Trevor and Cronofy, are dedicated solely to helping educators save time and optimize and automate key calendar dates and scheduling tasks. Trevor can be used as a day planner, allowing for the creation of time blocks and to-do lists. Cronofy offers timetable management in addition to lesson planning tools and AI-based teachers' assistants and can even be used for institutional admissions procedures. The overall goal of these advanced tools is to streamline time-sucking processes and protocols, freeing up more time to do what we do best: teach!

## IMPROVING COMMUNICATION

Effective communication habits drive the education experience, allowing us to collaborate closely with administrators, colleagues, parents, and students. Keeping the lines of communication open at all times presents significant challenges for us, however, because we can't be "on call" all the time, and the nature of teaching work itself demands so many out-of-classroom hours already.

Writing up personalized updates and report cards is time-consuming, plus the fact that we also have helicopter parents to contend with. There's a distinct need for more streamlined, efficient ways of going about managing the daily communication tasks we have as educators. The fact that the sheer volume of our responsibilities can get in the way of dedicating time to crafting personalized feedback and fielding parental concerns means that we need to seek better ways of alleviating some of this burden.

While there's some concern that automating any part of teacher communication could make things sound generic, the heavy weight of other tasks we face can often make this the case anyway. What AI-powered notifications can do is act as our virtual teacher's assistants, shooting out reminders, commendations, and warnings while we sleep.

If you're wondering what the applications of this type of AI-enabled notification system might be, here are a few ideas:

- **Reminders and alerts:** Routine reminders and warnings, such as those related to attendance or behavior issues, can be sent out to parents. This can also include scheduling reminders, such as those about upcoming field trips or extracurricular offerings.
- **Personalized feedback:** Automated notification systems, when armed with student data and metrics, can process and send out grades, feedback, and report cards automatically. Through data analytics, and the generation of user-friendly reports, parents can get quick-sheet overviews of their children's progress, making them feel more empowered and involved in the educational track.
- **Updates and milestones reached:** While we already discussed the gamification of educational tools a bit, it's important to note that one of the most effective aspects of these AI-fueled tools is that they use rewards and incentives to encourage learning. Automated notification systems integrated into learning and classroom management platforms can let parents know when their kids have a breakthrough moment, and when they get a stellar grade.

### Apps For Classroom Communication

### ClassDojo

ClassDojo is a social messaging app that connects teachers with parents, based on Social-Emotional learning principles. Breaking down classroom subjects and achievements into categories including Points, Big Ideas, and student Portfolios, it provides an accessible way for parents to know more about what students are studying and achieving in their classrooms. It also translates messages into up to 35 languages, making it a great tool for school districts that have a diverse, multilingual student and parent base. The best part: It's totally free to teachers and has a growing user base of over 50 million parents and students. For more information, check it out at: https://www.classdojo.com/

**ParentSquare**

ParentSquare connects classrooms and school services to communities through a number of direct notification, voice, and text messaging services that have two-way translation in over 100 languages. From classroom posts to message board updates and sign-up forms, the app offers a multitude of useful tools for both parents and teachers. It offers several valuable features that make it easier to update and correct parent contact information, ensuring that its helpful messages are received.

## RESOURCE ALLOCATION

Managing resources effectively is a key facet of effective teaching. Educators too often, especially in the United States, find themselves having to juggle between roles that are in the job description and other tasks that are required of us, unfortunately, due to budget shortfalls or other factors. We're expected to perform a continuous juggling of tasks, balancing lesson planning, creating high-quality education materials, and sometimes even having to buy classroom supplies on our dime. While what's expected of us is too much, we often feel pressure to give our classroom the best despite factors beyond our control. This especially rings true for those of us who are public educators in underserved school districts.

All the effort we put into the sourcing of material for the classroom too often goes unappreciated; however, this doesn't mean that we don't deserve better. In fact: We do! That's why it's important to start looking at the way AI-fueled automation could potentially help us out with making sure the resources we need are within arm's reach.

There's no reason we should be wasting our time managing things like classroom supply inventory when data and predictive analysis can automatically replenish the supplies and items we need. This also applies to time-wasting tasks like printing and copying. Who wants to stand over a Xerox all day preparing study packets, or putting together complex multi-page syllabi? Let's take a look at some other potential applications for this kind of powerful automation engine:

**Teaching materials and resources:** The great thing about AI-powered learning systems and classroom tools is that they give us a way to anticipate and plan for the teaching materials and resources we need throughout the academic year based on historical data from past years, along with current learning trends throughout educational institutions worldwide. These types of data-rich systems connect institutions of all levels worldwide to a centralized knowledge bank that enables schools and teachers to stay up-to-speed about the latest pedagogical approaches without having to read studies or journals. This helps ensure that students are receiving the best and most up-to-date information, and having it delivered to them in the most effective way, leaving room for the evolution of in-class activities and teaching methods over time.

**Supply management:** Institutional logistics and the ordering of materials, tools, and coordination of any outside vendors schools rely on are handled by a dedicated planning officer or administrator rather than teachers. For smaller schools especially, however, you may find yourself doing double duty at times, wondering how you ended up negotiating the price of milk cartons for school lunches when you have a million other things on your hands, including working on lesson plans and providing individualized attention and learning plans for your students. Whether the school you work in is big or small, it's important to know that there are a number of inventory management systems specifically built for schools, some incorporating powerful AI tools.

### *Supply Management Systems For Schools*

### Sortly

Sortly is a comprehensive inventory and asset management solution that works across all devices, from teachers' smartphones to administrators' personal computers, making it possible for all staff members to know where any tool or supply is at any given time. This doesn't only extend to items that are purchased and stocked, like #2 pencils and art supplies; it also extends to equipment, like computers, projectors, TVs, and any other A/V equipment that's common in classrooms.

The handy barcoding capability makes it easy to tag any inventory item, from beakers in the science lab to gym equipment, and even special items like decorations and banners that only come out once a year. The overall goal is to make sure that school staff know where any given item is at any given time, saving vast amounts of time spent tracking down objects.

While the Sortly management system doesn't have AI tools integrated itself, it has a public API, which means that enterprise customers are free to implement their own custom deployments of the software, including integrating it together with any custom AI solutions they have in place. This would mean, for instance, that algorithms could be used to anticipate future needs and generate useful reports on data gathered about inventory needs. It would also be able to perform audits that software inventory management systems like Sortly might not be capable of performing on their own.

**ASAP Systems**

ASAP Systems is another versatile and comprehensive inventory and asset management solution. Tailored specifically for the dynamic needs of schools and colleges, this system simplifies the management of a wide range of educational assets and resources.

At the heart of ASAP Systems is the software's capability to ensure the optimal maintenance and utilization of educational equipment, extending the product lifecycle and helping cut down on waste. It adeptly handles the scheduling of regular maintenance for various assets, ensuring they remain in prime condition. This proactive feature is crucial in educational settings, where the functionality of laboratory apparatus, computers, and A/V equipment is essential for daily learning activities.

A significant aspect of ASAP Systems is its efficient process for checking out and checking in educational assets and equipment. In a busy, hectic school environment, where resources like textbooks, lab equipment, and technology devices are constantly in use, the system seamlessly manages their circulation. This feature ensures that items are returned in a timely manner and remain in good condition, ready for the next user.

ASAP Systems is excellent at managing assets across multiple sites, a common scenario in larger educational institutions with multiple campuses or satellite locations. Whether tracking a set of science lab tools or a library book, the system keeps a vigilant eye on the whereabouts of each item. This comprehensive item-tracking capability is invaluable in preventing loss and ensuring the efficient use of resources across various departments and locations.

While ASAP Systems may not have AI tools directly embedded in its software, its robust framework allows for potential integration with AI-driven solutions used in educational settings. This could offer schools predictive analytics on inventory needs, and advanced data analysis, further automating and streamlining asset management tasks.

## AI IN LEARNING MANAGEMENT SYSTEMS (LMS)

Learning Management Systems (LMS) have become indispensable tools for today's most cutting-edge educational institutions. These systems serve as digital platforms for a range of purposes, from managing courses and curricula to tracking student progress and performance. The integration of AI into these systems has opened new avenues for enhancing the educational experience, both for educators and learners.

LMS platforms provide a structured online interface where educators can create, deliver, and manage educational content, and where students can access this content, submit assignments, and engage in discussions. They also facilitate the tracking of student progress, an essential aspect of personalized learning. As comprehensive as these systems are, their functionalities can be turbo-charged with the inclusion of powerful AI tools.

AI integration in LMS can transform these systems from just serving as repositories and trackers of educational content into dynamic tools that adapt and respond to the individual needs of students. AI can personalize the learning experience. Based on the data gathered, the system can recommend additional resources, suggest areas for improvement, and even adjust the difficulty level of assignments and quizzes to suit the learner's pace and understanding. This level of personalization ensures that each student receives an education tailored to their individual learning style and pace, promoting a more effective and engaging learning environment.

One of the key areas where AI has already made substantial improvements is in the automation of grading and assessment. AI-powered LMS can evaluate assignments and tests, providing instant feedback to students. This saves valuable time for educators while also helping ensure timely and consistent evaluation and the upholding of grading standards.

## STUDENT BEHAVIOR AND CLASSROOM MANAGEMENT

One of the most challenging parts of being a teacher is that we're often charged with managing student behaviors in the classroom. Behavioral issues can range from minor disruptions to more significant challenges that impact the learning environment for all students. Let's face it: Nobody wants to be a cop, but making sure the classroom is under control is often an important aspect of effectively managing K-12 educational environments. Traditional classroom behavior management strategies in these settings often include the following:

- setting clear expectations
- positive reinforcement
- consistent consequences

While these approaches have been shown to work, they can be time-consuming and sometimes are ineffective for certain students.

The advent of AI technology in the education sector offers new solutions to these longstanding challenges. AI can assist teachers in monitoring and managing student behavior more effectively and efficiently.

By analyzing data on student interactions and engagement, AI monitoring systems can identify patterns of behavior that may require intervention. This proactive approach enables teachers to address issues before they escalate, creating a more positive and proactive learning environment. AI technology reshapes classroom management by providing teachers with tools that make them more productive while helping students thrive.

One way that AI can help classroom behavioral issues and dynamics is by automating administrative tasks related to behavior management, such as recording incidents and tracking progress on behavior goals. This automation frees up time to focus on instruction and individual student needs.

Innovative AI applications like ChatGPT and Blackboard Learn offer practical tools for classroom management. Let's take a look at how to use them:

**ChatGPT Prompts**

Warnings and more subtle reminders generated by LLMs can guide teachers in creating effective communication strategies for addressing behavior issues and sending behavior reports to parents. Here are some examples of prompts you can try with ChatGPT, Google Bard, or other similar chat-based AI tools:

- Write a sensitively worded letter to Jimmy's mother letting her know that her child is drawing disturbing images in art class and that he might benefit from seeing the school counselor to talk about his feelings.

- Write a curt but polite text message to Sally's father letting him know that she received an in-school suspension for slamming a boy's hand in a locker, and he can pick her up from the vice principal's office from 2 pm onward.
- Write a letter in a courteous but firm matter to Alexandra's mother telling her that her daughter has missed 7:45 am roll call and the recitation of the pledge of allegiance every day this semester.
- Write an informal text message to Oscar's mother letting her know that he's getting much better about not interrupting other students during class and that it's a pleasure to have him in the classroom.

If your classroom is really out of control, and you've tried everything, you can also try asking one of these AI chatbots what to do. Here are some examples of prompts you might try:

- How can I improve the dynamics of my [insert grade] classroom?
- What fun activities can I plan to pull out of the magic hat when my [insert grade] classroom is being hyperactive and inattentive?
- If none of my [insert grade] students follow my instructions because my pleas for attention get drowned out in shrieks and screams, what can I do to improve my communication skills?

**Blackboard Learn by Anthology**

Blackboard Learn, made by the educational technology service company Anthology, provides a comprehensive system for tracking student engagement while driving participation in educational activities, helping both students and teachers achieve their goals.

The platform incorporates cloud-based SaaS delivery models to give users access no matter where they are, providing opportunities for personalized learning approaches and collaborative virtual environments.

Blackboard is available in a number of different packages and configurations, like the Lean Ultra solution, which won a Gold level International Business Award in 2022, and a Platinum award from Campus Technology's New Product Awards that same year. For more information, visit:

https://www.anthology.com/discover/anthology-learning-management/.

## INFUSING CHATGPT AND AI INTO THE WRITING PROCESS

Incorporating chat-based AI tools like ChatGPT or Google Bard into the production of original classroom content or allowing them to be used in student-written works, requires some careful consideration.

For both teachers and students, AI can serve as a powerful aid. You might be wondering: *Hey, that's cheating though!* Well, when used properly, it's certainly not. Here are a few ideas to get your brain juices flowing about how these much-hyped generative AI tools can make their way into your classroom:

**For Teachers**

- They can help teachers streamline outlining and document creation tasks.
- They can help speed up communication with parents and administrators, through the use of well-considered and well-crafted prompts.

**For All Subject Matters**

- They can be used as a substitute for flashcards on various subjects, as much as their training data allows for.

**English**

- They can help students gain better writing skills.
- They're great to use for class-wide brainstorming exercises and activities for writing projects.
- They can assist teachers in giving demonstrations about the structure of essays through a series of on-the-fly prompts about the various sections, from the Introduction to the Conclusion.
- They can be used as a language translator to assist ESL students.

## Science

- They can be used to conduct virtual chemistry or physics experiments that are made into quick in-class lab reports, so students learn the proper format and method of this type of written report.
- They can provide tutoring in scientific subjects, including biology.
- They can generate computer code.

## Math

- They're great as a virtual math tutor.
- They can be used as a talking calculator.
- They can explain complex mathematical concepts using easy-to-understand analogies.

As you can see, the practical uses are vast, as the ones I've laid out here just scratch the surface. That said, the usage of these tools, both in and outside the classroom, demands a careful approach to ensure ethical practices and to maintain academic integrity.

To ensure the ethical use of any AI tool in writing assignments specifically, certain best practices should be abided by. Here are the most important ones to keep in mind:

- **Don't encourage students to rely on AI for research:** The data could be inaccurate, incomplete, or out-of-date. While it's fine for outlining concepts, any facts, especially any that include numbers and statistics should be fact-checked and duly cited from a legitimate source.

- **Check for bias and educate your students on it:** The data that LLMs are trained on is never perfect, and it can lead to bias and misconceptions. If something doesn't sound right to you, check it out, and you might find an AI error at fault. Educate your students on the possibility of biased or incorrect information, making sure they develop good AI literacy skills.

- **The use of AI without disclosure is grounds for a failing grade:** If you tell students that a specific writing assignment should be done without the use of these tools, and you find out that they violated this specification, don't be afraid to give them a big F, and if you're generous, allow them a second chance to rewrite and resubmit the paper.

- **Be clear about what constitutes plagiarism:** While things are ever-changing when it comes to the issue of intellectual property in AI training data, and the attribution of original works, the bottom line is that most of the popular AI chatbots have been trained on lots of data that *is* under copyright protection. This means that they're liable to repeat parts of this data, either verbatim or in a way that closely resembles this work. This by most standards would constitute plagiarism, and if you use raw AI output without modifying it, the odds of accidental plagiarism increase. Let your students know this is not acceptable.

## *To Sum Things Up*

Generative AI tools like ChatGPT offer educators and students a whole new world of possibilities, particularly in the area of writing. That said, their use demands a balanced approach that focuses on enhancing the learning experience while also making sure to uphold best practices.

The value of original thinking needs to be emphasized, making sure both students and teachers realize that the power of these tools lies in their ability to further our own ideas, and enhance and streamline our original ways of communicating concepts and themes.

Another essential thing to remember is that these chat-based tools are fun. In the next chapter, we'll be talking all about classroom engagement, so get ready to see how we can use AI tools to create engaging and enjoyable content for the classroom!

# 8

# ENHANCING STUDENT ENGAGEMENT

Today's digitally enabled world provides us with a plethora of opportunities, but it has also threatened to fundamentally alter the wiring of our brains. Consider the fact that Canadian researchers found that since the year 2000, the average person's attention span has diminished from 12 seconds to 8 seconds, making our ability to focus less than that of a goldfish (McSpadden, 2015). This shocking statistic points to the fact that both teachers and students, due to our ever-increasing use of screens and mobile devices, need to be engaged in ways that are tailored toward our diminished capacities for sustained attention.

AI represents one way we can tackle this issue, giving us new ways of approaching classroom engagement. In this chapter, we'll take a look at how AI-powered educational tools, including game-based study platforms, interactive lesson generators, and creative aids like generative graphics can help inspire our classrooms, while also reinvigorating our passion for teaching.

While many of the tools we'll be looking at have strange-sounding names, from Kahoot to Nearpod and Socrative, many of these useful platforms and apps promise to become household names as these advanced tools are further integrated into our educational system. So, let's dive right in and start discovering the tools of a promising new future that are poised to bring us a more interactive, more personalized, and more engaging educational experience.

## MAKING CLASSES MORE FUN WITH GAME-BASED LEARNING

Game-based learning has been a part of classroom learning for some time now, helping kids practice math, develop their vocabulary, and more recently even help with foreign language studies. While more traditional instruction methods have a high value in all of these disciplines, rote learning often fails to address individual student concerns and learning trajectories, further compounding the problem we face today with the attention spans of our students, and let's face it: our own attention spans as well.

This is where the power of game-based learning tools emerges as a promising way for already screen-addicted students to get excited about the subject matter they wouldn't normally be so enthralled by. Through gamification, we can deliver rich content through a saccharine-sweet delivery method that satisfies our students' limitless craving for novelty, games, and more rapid-fire approaches to learning and studying that reward them when they do well.

### Game-Based Educational Tools

While there are a ton of game-based educational tools out there, Prodigy and Kahoot stand as particularly good examples of what these types of systems can offer.

### Prodigy

Prodigy is an AI-powered platform that transforms math and English into an exciting role-playing game that provides learning paths for students up to eighth-grade level. It engages students with challenges tailored to their individual learning needs, making tricky subjects like algebra and grammar both fun and accessible.

In the math learning game they offer, students are able to choose wizard avatars that inhabit a magical world. As you might guess, solving math problems is key to racking up points and advancing in the game.

In the English subject matter game, the theme is world-building, and students are able to progress through the game by answering questions that allow them to mine resources and collect the materials necessary to build new worlds.

Whichever subject matter you choose, whether math or English, Prodigy makes learning an adventure rather than a chore.

**Kahoot**

Kahoot brings quiz-show-like excitement into the classroom. Teachers can use it to create customized quizzes related to their curriculum, and students participate in these lively, competitive games using their devices. Kahoot's real-time feedback and playful format make learning a social and enjoyable activity, encouraging participation and boosting knowledge retention.

Boasting an AI-based content generator, teachers can use this tool to speed up their process by helping them develop the questions. It's not just fun, as according to Kahoot's claims, it can help increase focus and motivation.

Kahoot has business applications too, and its use doesn't only extend to in-class activities. It could be great for after-school programs and teacher summits and could be great for school-wide special events such as dances and fundraising events. It could even be brought along on field trips running on mobile devices.

## AI TOOLS FOR INTERACTIVE LESSONS

The enhancement of student engagement through interactive lessons is a growing facet of modern education. By shifting away from the traditional lecture format to a more dynamic and participatory model, educators committed to these new pedagogical approaches can foster a learning environment that captivates and maintains students' attention.

AI-driven tools, such as Nearpod and Socrative, are at the forefront of this educational revolution. These platforms allow teachers to create interactive presentations and in-class exercises that encourage higher levels of classroom participation.

## Nearpod

Nearpod is a versatile tool that empowers educators to bring their lessons to life. It offers features like immersive Virtual Reality (VR), quizzes, and interactive videos, enabling educators to create lessons that are not only informative but also immersive. Nearpod's AI capabilities allow teachers to speed up lesson preparation time and help them increase the personalization of lesson content, ensuring that the needs of diverse learners are met. The interactive experience it offers helps keep students engaged and helps teachers have less work in driving this engagement.

## Socrative

Socrative, another powerful AI tool, elevates the traditional quiz format into an interactive learning experience. Teachers can create real-time quizzes, polls, and games that encourage student participation. Socrative's instant feedback system is particularly effective, as it enables students to understand their progress and areas of improvement immediately. This immediate feedback loop keeps students actively involved in their learning process and allows teachers to adjust their instruction in real time based on student responses, and helps teachers give grades with ease.

## BOOSTING CREATIVITY THROUGH AI

In today's educational landscape, making sure that kids come out of their K-12 years with a capacity for creative thinking is a necessity. The proliferation of AI tools itself signals that the human ability to be truly creative will continue to be a necessity. Rather than replace our innate abilities to imagine new things, AI tools can help boost and focus human creativity, from speeding up brainstorming, to creating models and mockups of our original ideas that aid us in realizing them.

AI-enhanced platforms like Canva and Plotagon are revolutionizing the way educational content is created, making it more engaging, visually appealing, and conducive to creative exploration.

**Canva**

Canva offers a plethora of design options that teachers can use to create visually stunning presentations, infographics, and educational materials using a wide variety of intuitive, expertly designed templates. Its interface is easy to navigate, and it allows educators to express their creativity by creating advanced and professional-looking multimedia for the classroom without needing to have any advanced graphic design skills themselves.

**Plotagon**

Plotagon offers educators an innovative way to engage students through animated storytelling that operates off a text-to-animation AI technology. Through the app, teachers and students can create animated videos, simulating real-life scenarios or historical events, thereby enhancing learning through a creative and interactive medium. This not only aids in better understanding and retention of information but also encourages students to think out of the box. While they may also use this tool to make some unsavory content or to bully other students, the benefits far outweigh the potential for abuse.

## MONITORING ENGAGEMENT WITH AI TOOLS

Understanding and maintaining student engagement can be one of the most challenging parts of effective teaching. In a classroom, whether virtual or physical, gauging student interest and participation is necessary for educators to ensure effective learning. The problem often lies in how we go about achieving this, as monitoring student engagement poses significant challenges.

Traditional methods of measuring engagement, such as observing student behavior or relying on participation, can be subjective and often miss the more subtle signs of disengagement.

The advent of AI tools offers a new dimension to this challenge. AI-driven platforms like Classcraft and GoGuardian are revolutionizing how educators monitor and enhance student engagement. These tools use sophisticated algorithms to track various indicators of engagement in real time, providing educators with valuable insights that were previously difficult to obtain.

While we don't want children to feel like they're under constant surveillance, and ethics questions arise, the benefits of the useful metrics and other data these tools offer far outweigh any of these factors. This makes them great choices for educational institutions taking a personalized approach to learning.

**Classcraft**

Classcraft is a behavioral management tool that educators can use to drive classroom motivation while monitoring for behavioral issues, and noting student progress and milestones. By using gamification principles that encourage positive behavior, the system allows students to get creative by choosing their own avatars and awards them with experience points for good behavior.

Educators who use the system can expect to receive early intervention data that can help target special attention toward those in need of positive motivation and individualized emotional attention. The tool gives teachers the ability to gain quantifiable metrics on the engagement level of their students, providing them with useful starting points for identifying and taking the steps to solve behavioral and attention deficits. And the best part? It's fully integrable with other common learning tools including Clever, ClassLink, Canvas, and Google Classroom.

**GoGuardian**

While Classcraft focuses more on rewarding positive behavior and empowering teachers to intervene, GoGuardian takes a harder-line approach to classroom surveillance and monitoring. Its list of features includes in-class filtering and monitoring of computers and mobile devices, allowing teachers to peer into the world of inappropriate content that students often seek out, and allows teachers to actively block content, giving them a way to take a more proactive approach to monitoring what their students see and have access to.

GoGuardian's digital surveillance and monitoring tools aren't just to make sure students aren't viewing inappropriate content, as the ultimate goal is to take away any potential for distractions that could potentially impede lesson delivery. While GoGuardian may seem like a digital police officer in some ways, the ultimate goal is student safety; and that's why there are integrated tools for alerting teachers and administrators about the potential for suicide or self-harm. While the ramifications of such technology have implications for student privacy issues, the ultimate goal is a positive one, which is monitoring the mental health of the student body, and ensuring that all students make responsible choices during school hours.

### Before We Move On

As we've seen, it's evident that AI tools are poised to continue enhancing the educational experience by making classes more engaging while also focusing on cutting down on distractions and ensuring a safe learning environment for all. Through innovative AI-driven solutions such as game-based learning platforms, interactive lesson tools, creativity boosters, and digital behavior monitoring tools, education is being transformed into an engaging and dynamic process that caters to the unique needs and interests of each student.

As is the case with any AI tool, especially those decisions that could affect their learning trajectory and outcomes, it's crucial to recognize the responsibilities that accompany the use of such advanced technology. That's why in the next chapter, we'll be diving deep into the ethical implications and responsibilities that come with integrating AI into education. The question of how to balance the advantages of AI with the necessity of maintaining ethical standards is one of the most pressing ones we deal with today as these systems become ever-more prevalent in our classrooms. Finding the right balance between technology and ethical consideration is the way that we can ensure going forward that the use of AI in education remains both highly beneficial and responsible.

# 9

# STAYING AHEAD

For better or for worse, the role of a modern educator is one that transcends traditional boundaries and job descriptions, having transformed into one of being a future-readiness coach for student success. It's a role that demands not just foresight but also a deep understanding and embrace of the technological waves shaping our world.

The question we face now, as passionate educators on the brink of great change, isn't whether AI will have a role in education's future, but how quickly we'll accept the fact that it has arrived and will become a mature technology before we know it. What this means is that it's important to be prepared to harness its power both effectively and responsibly.

How do we, as educators, prepare ourselves and our students for a world increasingly influenced by AI? This chapter is all about how to choose, deploy, and consider the ethical ramifications of AI tools in education, equipping us with the necessary toolkit to navigate today's turbo tech-charged educational landscape confidently and competently.

## CHOOSING THE BEST AI TOOLS

As educators, we face a great responsibility when it comes to selecting the right AI tools to implement in our classrooms. While in some cases, it may be dictated to us by administration or may fall under certain district-wide restrictions—for many of us the wide range of options before us can be daunting. We're charged with finding the right AI tools that resonate with our teaching style and the educational goals we've set for our classroom, and also address the unique needs of our students. The right selection of specific AI tools and their applied implementation can spell the difference between continued frustration and success.

When it comes to selecting what AI tools to demo, several important factors come into play. First, it's important to remember that ease of use from your end is paramount. If you don't understand how to use a tool right away, spend some time with it. If it still doesn't click with you, this may be a sign to move on to assessing the next one.

One thing that's certain is that tools that are intuitive and user-friendly reduce the learning curve for both teachers and students, ensuring a smoother integration into the classroom environment. Another factor to consider is the cost of any AI-powered classroom tool or learning platform. Budget constraints in educational settings necessitate finding solutions that offer the best value without compromising on quality, and depending on what type of school you work in, there may not be a budget at all.

Lastly, the effectiveness of these tools in achieving desired educational outcomes is another area that needs to be assessed. Remember: Any AI tool you choose to try out in your classroom should enhance, rather than detract from, the overall educational experience.

To aid in this selection process, here are some top-rated AI tools, categorized by their primary uses in the classroom. Note that an asterisk will be used to mark the ones already covered in previous chapters, so you can easily refer back to those for more details.

### Personalized Learning and Tutoring

- **DreamBox\*:** An adaptive learning platform that provides personalized math learning. It intelligently adjusts to each student's learning pace and style, offering interactive math problems and activities.
- **Woot Math:** Tailors math instruction to individual student needs. It offers adaptive learning environments and hands-on, interactive math activities to improve students' understanding of mathematical concepts.
- **TutorMe:** An online tutoring platform that connects students with personal tutors across various subjects. It offers one-on-one learning sessions, ensuring tailored instruction.
- **Duolingo:** A popular language learning app that uses gamification and AI to offer personalized language

lessons. It adapts to the learner's style and progress, making language learning engaging and effective.

- **Stepwise Math:** Helps students learn math through step-by-step instructions and problem-solving exercises. It's designed to assist students at various learning levels, simplifying complex math problems.

### *Classroom Management and Engagement*

- **Classcraft\*:** An educational role-playing game that transforms classroom management into a game, increasing student engagement and motivation.
- **GoGuardian\*:** A tool for managing and monitoring student activities online. It helps ensure safe internet usage in schools and provides analytics on student engagement.
- **ClassDojo\*:** A communication app that connects educators with students and parents. It allows for the sharing of reports, photos, and videos from the classroom in real time.
- **Involvio:** A comprehensive student engagement platform that tracks and improves student engagement and campus life through AI-driven insights.
- **Classtime:** Offers interactive classroom activities and quizzes. It facilitates engaging, collaborative learning experiences and real-time assessment.
- **iClassPro:** Manages class scheduling, attendance, and communication with students and parents. It's designed for a variety of class-based businesses, including educational ones.

- **Classter:** Provides a comprehensive suite of tools for educational and administrative management, integrating student information with learning and classroom management.
- **myday:** A student engagement platform with integrated communication tools that are targeted toward small and midsize enterprise customers and higher education institutions.
- **MobileUp:** A student engagement platform that's designed for agencies and startups that can provide orientation and higher education services.
- **Schoox:** A learning management system for various educational needs designed for small to midsize enterprise customers.
- **Campus Labs:** A student engagement platform designed for small to midsize enterprise customers and agencies.

### Assessment and Testing

- **Eklavvya:** An online platform providing a suite of tools for digital assessments, including exams and quizzes, with AI-driven analytics and cheating prevention measures.
- **Kahoot\*:** A game-based learning platform used to create educational quizzes and interactive lessons. It increases engagement and makes learning fun.
- **Prodigy\*:** A math game-based learning platform that aligns with curriculum standards. It offers a compelling

learning experience through interactive math challenges.

- **Socrative\*:** An interactive tool that enables educators to create quizzes, polls, and games that stimulate student engagement and provide instant feedback.

### Content Creation and Lesson Planning

- **Canva\*:** An intuitive design tool that educators can use to create visually appealing educational materials like presentations, worksheets, and infographics.
- **Plotagon\*:** Allows users to create animated videos using AI. It's useful for creating engaging educational content and storytelling.
- **Nearpod\*:** Enables interactive lesson delivery with features like quizzes, polls, and VR. It makes lessons more engaging and provides instant feedback.
- **Adobe Express & Fotor AI:** Tools for creating high-quality visual content for educational purposes, from infographics to class presentations.
- **Slidesgo:** Offers AI-powered templates for presentations, helping educators create professional-looking slides quickly and easily.
- **Altitude Learning:** A platform designed for lesson planning and personalization; it integrates learning objectives with student-centric approaches.
- **Firefly:** Helps educators with lesson planning and classroom management, offering tools to create, set, and mark homework, quizzes, and more.

## Data Analytics and Monitoring

- **Smart Sparrow:** Provides adaptive eLearning tools that offer analytics on student performance and engagement, helping educators tailor their teaching.
- **Edmentum:** Offers a wide range of educational content and assessment tools, complete with data analytics for tracking student progress.
- **Top Hat:** Specializes in student engagement and performance analytics, offering interactive teaching tools and real-time feedback mechanisms.

## Communication and Collaboration

- **ParentSquare*:** A unified school-to-home communication platform that ensures parents are informed and involved in their children's education.
- **Signal Vine:** Offers personalized messaging and communication solutions, enabling tailored outreach to students based on their individual needs.
- **CampusGroups:** Manages student groups and activities, enhancing campus life and student engagement through a centralized platform.

*Educational Services & Miscellaneous*

- **Pearson:** Provides a wide array of educational tools and resources, including textbooks, online learning solutions, and assessment services.
- **Wise - Lead Management:** A tool designed for managing student inquiries and admissions, streamlining the process of lead management in educational institutions.
- **Skyward Student Management:** A comprehensive K-12 student information system that helps manage student data, including grades, attendance, and health records.
- **HDSchool:** A school management platform for student records, attendance, library check-outs, and more.
- **Sortly\*:** An inventory management software tailored for educational settings, helping manage supplies and resources efficiently.
- **ASAP Systems\*:** Offers inventory and asset tracking solutions specifically designed for educational environments, ensuring efficient resource management.
- **CampusNexus:** A cloud-based student data and campus management system.

## IMPLEMENTING AI TOOLS IN THE CLASSROOM

Implementing AI tools in the classroom should be carried out in a well-considered, gradual way. It's a process that requires careful planning, collaboration, and a willingness to adapt on-the-fly. Let's walk through the key steps to ensure a smooth and effective implementation of AI technology.

### The Initial Planning Phase

- **Clearly define your goals:** Start by writing down what you aim to achieve with AI in your classroom. Whether it's enhancing student engagement, personalizing learning, or improving assessment methods, having clear objectives before you start browsing the latest tools and solutions will help you focus your decision-making approaches and strategies.
- **Research the tools appropriate for your use case:** Don't be afraid to dive right into researching the latest in today's AI-fueled educational tools. Explore various options, be mindful of any budgetary considerations that might narrow your search, read reviews, and most importantly: Understand the features of each tool. It's essential to choose tools that align with your teaching goals and the needs of your students.
- **Brainstorm your envisioned usage:** Assess the potential implementation and impacts of the AI tools you're considering. Think about how it can aid in your teaching while supporting your students' learning. Consider factors like ease of use, cost, compatibility with existing systems, and the learning curve required for you and your students.

*Getting the Green Light and Going Forward*

- **Involve others:** Engage with fellow educators, administrators, and potentially even parents and students to get their input and validation. Discuss how the AI tools can benefit the classroom and address any concerns they may have.
- **Soft-launch the AI tools:** Before a full-scale implementation, conduct a pilot test. Choose a small group of students or a particular class to test the tools. This approach allows you to gauge the effectiveness of the system and then make any necessary adjustments before the full rollout.

*The Rollout*

- **Implement the tools:** Once you have tested and are comfortable with the AI tools, begin integrating them into your daily teaching practices.
- **Provide opportunities for training:** Ensure that you, your students, and your parents are adequately trained in using the AI tools. This could include tutorial sessions to familiarize everyone with the functionalities and best practices.
- **Be clear about data privacy policies:** If you teach outside of an institution that has its own data privacy policy, or are a freelance instructor or adjunct faculty member at a non-conventional or non-formalized school, you may consider having your students sign a waiver. This way you won't be held legally liable for any

misunderstandings around what the AI systems you use in your classroom do using their data.

- **Monitor progress:** Keep an eye on how the tools are impacting your teaching and your students' learning. Use analytics to glean rich data, and rely on feedback to assess whether your initial goals are being met.

## Tracking Progress

- **Gather feedback regularly:** Make a habit of collecting feedback from students, other faculty members, and parents. Understanding their experiences will provide valuable insights into the effectiveness of the AI tools.
- **Stay updated:** The field of AI in education is rapidly evolving. Stay informed about the latest developments, updates to existing tools you're using, and any new emerging technologies that could further enhance your teaching.

With a bit of visionary foresight, careful planning, open communication, and a dedicated commitment to continuous learning and improvement, you can arrive at an AI solution that works for you and your students. By following these guidelines, you'll be able to effectively harness the power of AI to enrich your teaching and provide your students with a more engaging and personalized learning experience.

## INSTILLING ETHICAL AI USE IN STUDENTS

The more we start incorporating AI in the classroom, the more important it becomes to instill a strong foundation of ethical AI use. This goes beyond just conveying responsible use from a practical standpoint, as it also includes sensitive concepts such as privacy, data security, and the broader implications of AI on society.

### The Importance of Ethical AI Use

- **Privacy and data security:** In an era where data breaches are common, it's critical to teach students the importance of data privacy and security in AI applications. They should understand how AI systems use data and be aware of the importance of protecting their own personal and sensitive information.
- **Responsible use:** Students need to be aware of the potential impacts of AI on people and society. This includes understanding the inherent biases in AI systems, and the ethical considerations in utilizing AI in decision-making and student assessment tasks.

### Programs and Curricula for Ethical AI Education in Schools

- **Integrating AI ethics into existing curricula:** Schools and educators can integrate matters of AI ethics into various subjects. For instance, social studies teachers might discuss the societal impacts of AI, while a computer science professor might want to incorporate discussions about data privacy and algorithmic biases into lectures on technical aspects of programming.

- **Specialized AI ethics programs:** Some educational institutions have started offering specialized courses or modules focused on AI ethics. These programs aim to provide students with a comprehensive understanding of the ethical dimensions of AI technology. While nothing this formal is necessary, a certain level of training should be required for any wide-scale rollout of AI technology in school systems and individual institutions.
- **Project-based learning:** Encouraging students to engage in projects that require them to use AI ethically is an excellent way to instill these values. Projects could involve creating AI applications with a focus on fairness and privacy or analyzing case studies of AI use in various industries.

### The Role of the Teacher

- **Facilitated discussions:** Teachers can play a key role in AI ethics education by facilitating classroom discussions on the ethical implications of AI. This could involve debates, group discussions, and critical analysis of real-world AI use cases.
- **Provide resources and guidance:** Educators can provide students with resources such as articles, case studies, news broadcasts, and other types of exposés that explore the ethical dimensions of AI. Guiding

students in researching and understanding different perspectives on AI ethics is invaluable.

- **Stand as a model of ethical use:** Teachers should model ethical AI use in their teaching practices. This includes responsibly using AI tools in the classroom and being transparent about how the technology is used in educational settings.
- **Collaborate with AI experts:** Collaborating with people who work at the forefront of the field can enhance the quality of AI ethics education. Inviting guest speakers, organizing workshops, and participating in events focused on AI ethics can provide valuable learning experiences for both students and teachers.

By integrating these strategies into the classroom, educators can effectively prepare students to navigate the complex ethical landscape of AI. This makes sure they're equipped with the skills necessary to use the technology responsibly while also molding them into conscientious digital citizens in an increasingly AI-driven world.

## PREPARING FOR FUTURE AI TRENDS IN EDUCATION

As educators in a rapidly evolving technological landscape, it's crucial to not only adapt to current AI tools but also prepare for future trends that will shape the educational sector. Understanding and embracing these emerging trends will enable educators to stay ahead, ensuring that their teaching methods and curriculum remain relevant and effective.

*Emerging Trends in AI and Their Impact on Education*

- **Augmented Reality (AR) in Learning**: AR is transforming the educational experience by making learning more interactive and immersive. This technology can bring abstract concepts to life, providing students with a tangible and engaging way to understand complex subjects.
- **Blockchain for Credentialing**: Blockchain technology is poised to revolutionize how educational credentials are issued and verified. It offers a secure and transparent way to manage academic records, making it easier to verify qualifications and reduce fraudulent claims.
- **Personalized Learning through AI**: AI's ability to analyze vast amounts of data enables more personalized learning experiences. By understanding each student's unique learning style and pace, AI can tailor educational content to meet individual needs, thereby enhancing learning outcomes.
- **AI in Student Assessment and Feedback**: Future AI tools will likely provide more nuanced and accurate assessments of student performance. They will be able to analyze not just what students are learning, but how they are learning, offering real-time feedback and suggestions for improvement.

*Staying Updated with AI Trends in Education*

- **Follow TechEd publications and journals:** Educators should regularly follow reputable publications, journals, and online platforms that focus on educational technology and AI trends. These resources offer valuable insights into the latest developments and research in the field.
- **Attend webinars and conferences:** Participating in webinars and attending conferences on AI in education is an excellent way for educators to stay informed. These events often feature experts in the field and provide opportunities for networking and collaborative learning.
- **Consider professional development courses:** Many educational institutions and organizations offer professional development courses on AI and emerging technologies. These courses can help educators acquire new skills and understand how to integrate AI tools into their teaching.
- **Join online communities and forums:** Online communities and forums dedicated to AI in education can be great sources of information and support. These platforms allow educators to exchange ideas, share experiences, and learn from each other.
- **Experiment with new tools and technologies:** Hands-on experience with new AI tools and technologies is invaluable. Educators should be open to experimenting with emerging AI applications in their classrooms and

adapting their teaching methods to incorporate these tools effectively.

By actively engaging with these resources and staying abreast of emerging trends, we can prepare ourselves and our students for a future where AI plays a central role in education. This proactive approach enhances the learning experience while ensuring that we stay on the pulse of educational innovation.

## RESOURCES FOR TEACHERS AND STUDENTS WHO WANT TO KNOW MORE

In a landscape where AI is becoming increasingly integral to education, it's important for us to stay informed and skilled in its wide range of applications. To aid in this, a whole wealth of resources are within arm's reach, ranging from websites and online courses to books and specialized tools. Here's a compilation of valuable resources and tools that can help educators and their students become more comfortable with AI by learning about the underlying technologies behind it:

**Teachable Machine**

Teachable Machine is a fun, easy-to-use app that helps students *and* teachers learn about how machine learning algorithms work. It lets students create and train their own AI models that respond dynamically to feedback such as their own body movements and facial expressions. Check it out at: https://teachablemachine.withgoogle.com/

## Stretch AI

Stretch AI is a chatbot tool that's designed with one specific purpose in mind: educating educators on the pedagogical methods and approaches to incorporating AI into our classrooms. Think of Stretch AI as a digital Teacher's Assistant, helping you on your way toward integrating your perfect AI teaching system. It can field any questions or doubts you might have and provide great tips.

## Intel® AI for Youth

The chipmaker Intel's program is geared at high school students who want to take a crack at building their own AI models. This program, which is now available in countries all over the world, doesn't just teach the technical side, as there's also plenty of course material related to issues of data privacy, ethics, and responsible use. The course material is advanced enough to be exciting, but understandable enough to make it relatable, making it a great choice for teachers and students who want to know more.

## Coursera and edX

Online learning platforms such as Coursera and edX offer a range of courses on AI, many of which are suitable for educators of all different grade levels and subject matter. Courses cover the basics of AI, its applications in education, and more advanced topics for those looking to deepen their understanding of how to successfully incorporate these tools into their classrooms.

*To Sum Things Up*

By utilizing resources like these, teachers can enhance their professional development in the field of AI. Staying informed and skilled in AI applications is ultimately what will help us shape a future-ready education system that prepares students for the challenges and opportunities of a rapidly changing world.

Remember: At the core of all these discussions, tools, and techniques is your empowerment as an educator, and a citizen of the world charged with the weighty task of bringing up the next generation of curious thinkers. AI helps us make our roles as educators more impactful, keeps our classrooms more engaging, and helps make our careers more fulfilling.

As we conclude this final chapter, it's important to recall why all of this matters to *you*, as an educator, and how it shapes the future of those *you* teach. What's true for all of us committed, passionate educators is that the world of AI in education is something worth investing our time and energies in, and it's something that's here to stay.

# HELP OTHER TEACHERS STAY AT THE TOP OF THEIR GAME AND ACHIEVE A GOOD WORK-LIFE BALANCE

I hope you have already tried the myriad of AI tools and tips I shared in this book. My dream is for you to stay on top of your many tasks and for your students to achieve impressive results. If so, I would love it if you could share your thoughts and a little bit about your own story with other educators.

Simply by sharing your opinion about this book and how it has enriched your classes, you'll show them how AI can help them achieve the work-life balance they seek.

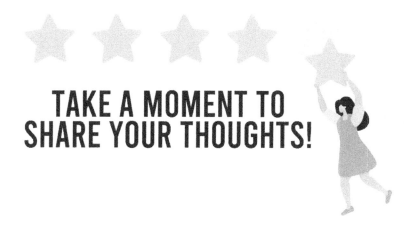

**TAKE A MOMENT TO SHARE YOUR THOUGHTS!**

Thank you so much for your support. I wish you the utmost fulfillment this profession can bring and your students the impressive results that arise from personalized, dynamic learning.

# Scan the QR code below

# CONCLUSION

As we reach the conclusion of this journey into the world of AI in education, it remains important to reflect on the core message of this book: AI is not just a fleeting trend in education but a transformative force that, when harnessed wisely, can profoundly enrich the teaching and learning experience.

Throughout the pages of this book, we've explored the vast potential of AI in various educational contexts, from automating administrative tasks and enhancing student engagement to emphasizing the importance of ethical AI use while anticipating and preparing for future trends. These insights collectively underscore the key takeaway: AI in education is a powerful tool, capable of revolutionizing how we teach, learn, and think about education.

But our deep dive into AI in education doesn't end with the closing of these pages. It's just the beginning. As educators, *we* have a unique opportunity to be pioneers in integrating AI into our own teaching strategies and methods, thereby shaping a future of education that is more efficient, engaging, and inclusive.

The future of education is being written now, and you have the power to influence its direction. Don't let the future leave you behind—start implementing AI tools in your teaching strategy today. Be the change-maker who harnesses the power of AI for a better tomorrow by driving improved student outcomes. Your commitment to adapting and embracing these changes can elevate your current teaching experience, while also inspiring and empowering your students for years to come.

If this book has provided you with valuable insights and guidance, please consider sharing your thoughts and experiences in a review. Your feedback is not only appreciated but will also help other educators navigate this exciting and evolving landscape of AI in education. So, go onward, continue to learn and grow, and let's transform education together toward a brighter AI-fueled future!

# REFERENCES

AIContentfy Team. (2023, July 5). *The ethics of using AI writing tools.* AIContentfy. https://aicontentfy.com/en/blog/ethics-of-using-ai-writing-tools

*A smart planner for academic professionals and tutors.* (n.d.). Trevor AI. Retrieved November 28, 2023, from https://trevorai.com/use-cases/academic-professionals

A T, R. (2020, April 11). *Why "one size fits all education" might not work anymore.* The Higher Education Review. https://www.thehighereducationreview.com/news/why-one-size-fits-all-education-might-not-work-anymore-nid-1326.html

Abeyta, M. (2023, May 29). *How AI helps Colorado instructors do more teaching: "What this does, in essence, is accesses excellent high-level information."* CBS Colorado. https://www.cbsnews.com/colorado/news/colorado-ai-helping-teachers-more-teaching/

Abd-Elaal, E.-S., Gamage, S., & Mills, J. (2019). *Artificial intelligence is a tool for cheating academic integrity.* https://aaee.net.au/wp-content/uploads/2020/07/AAEE2019_Annual_Conference_paper_180.pdf

*Academic and administrative role of AI in education.* (2022, April 20). Scholarly Community Encyclopedia. https://encyclopedia.pub/entry/21766

Academic Leadership. (2018, March 19). *The benefits and challenges of personalized learning.* Independent School Management. https://www.isminc.com/index.php/advisory/publications/the-source/benefits-and-challenges-personalized-learning

*Addressing teacher burnout: Causes, symptoms, and strategies | american university.* (2021, February 16). School of Education. https://soeonline.american.edu/blog/teacher-burnout/

Adlawan, D. (2023, May 22). *7 best AI tools for teachers everyone NEEDS to use in 2023.* Classpoint. https://blog.classpoint.io/best-ai-tools-for-teachers/

*AI accurately identifies normal and abnormal chest x-rays.* (2023, March 7). RSNA: Radiological Society of North America. https://www.rsna.org/news/2023/march/ai-identifies-normal-abnormal-xrays

*AI in education: 5 ways it can assist teachers.* (2022, November 17). ViewSonic

Library. https://www.viewsonic.com/library/education/ai-in-education-5-ways-it-can-assist-teachers/

*AI in finance: Applications, examples & benefits.* (n.d.). Google Cloud. https://cloud.google.com/discover/finance-ai

*AI-Based learning platform: Examples, features, and 5 top LMS to try | zavvy.* (2023, September 11). Zavvy. https://www.zavvy.io/blog/ai-based-lms

*AI-Based LMS: A guide to AI-powered learning platforms.* (2023, July 4). ProProfs Training Blog. https://www.proprofstraining.com/blog/ai-lms/

*AI-Powered lesson plan generator.* (n.d.). Auto Classmate. https://autoclassmate.io/tools/ai-powered-lesson-plan-generator/

*AI-Powered LMS (learning management system).* (n.d.). Softengi. https://softengi.com/blog/ai-blog/ai-powered-lms-learning-management-system/

*AI: Dos and don'ts in university education.* (2023, August 16). University of Iceland. https://english.hi.is/news/ai_dos_and_donts_in_university_education

AIContentfy Team. (2023, May 26). *The ethics of using AI content tools in writing.* AIContentfy. https://aicontentfy.com/en/blog/ethics-of-using-ai-content-tools-in-writing

Amato, N. (2015). *A lack of resources for many classrooms.* New York TImes. https://www.nytimes.com/roomfordebate/2015/03/26/is-improving-schools-all-about-money/a-lack-of-resources-for-many-classrooms

Anyoha, R. (2017, August 28). *The history of artificial intelligence.* Science in the News; Harvard University. https://sitn.hms.harvard.edu/flash/2017/history-artificial-intelligence/

Aparajeya Dash. (2016, November 11). *Failure of communication between teachers and students.* Toppr Bytes. https://www.toppr.com/bytes/failure-communication-between-teachers-and-students/

Applications of artificial intelligence across various industries. (2023, January 6). *Forbes.* https://www.forbes.com/sites/qai/2023/01/06/applications-of-artificial-intelligence/

Arampatzis, A. (n.d.). *Always learning: How AI prevents data breaches.* KDnuggets. https://www.kdnuggets.com/2023/07/always-learning-ai-prevents-data-breaches.html

arley, C. (2021, December 17). *10 benefits of personalized learning.* Oryx Learning. https://oryxlearning.com/learn/10-benefits-of-personalized-learning/

*Artificial intelligence in finance [15 examples].* (2021, April 2). University of San Diego. https://onlinedegrees.sandiego.edu/artificial-intelligence-finance/

Asling, D. (2020). *19 powerful ways to use artificial intelligence in eCommerce.* Linn Works. https://www.linnworks.com/blog/artificial-intelligence-in-ecommerce

Assefa, E. (2017, December 8). *The top six big data challenges in education.* SOMAmetrics. https://www.somametrics.com/top-six-big-data-challenges-education/

Baker Donelson. (2023, June 12). *AI in the classroom – new guidance from the department of education.* JD Supra. https://www.jdsupra.com/legalnews/ai-in-the-classroom-new-guidance-from-9118862/

Baraishuk, D. (2023, May 7). *AI in edtech: Top 15 edtech AI startups that won the market.* Belitsoft. https://belitsoft.com/custom-elearning-development/ai-in-education/ai-in-edtech

Barth, S. (2023). *Artificial intelligence (AI) in healthcare & hospitals.* ForeSee Medical. https://www.foreseemed.com/artificial-intelligence-in-healthcare

Bartram, F. (2022, January 4). *10 best AI chatbots for customer service performance (2022).* The CX Lead. https://thecxlead.com/tools/best-ai-chatbot-for-customer-service/

Blatchford, P., Brown, P., Bassett, P., & Koutsoubou, M. (2009, August). *Table 3 .1 -Administrative tasks carried out by teachers and support staff from Deployment and Impact of Support Staff in Schools The Impact of Support Staff in Schools (Results from Strand 2, Wave 2).* ResearchGate. https://www.researchgate.net/figure/1-Administrative-tasks-carried-out-by-teachers-and-support-staff_tbl2_267970842

Bogardus Cortez, M. (2017, August). *Teachers struggle with personalized learning initiatives, study finds.* Technology Solutions That Drive Education. https://edtechmagazine.com/k12/article/2017/08/teachers-struggle-personalized-learning-initiatives-study-finds

Bouchrika, I. (2020, August 19). *10 online education trends: 2021/2022 predictions, reports & data.* Research.com. https://research.com/education/online-education-trends

Bouchrika, I. (2022, July 21). *Teacher burnout: Challenges in K-12 and higher education.* Research.com. https://research.com/education/teacher-burnout-challenges-in-k-12-and-higher-education

Bowen, J. (2023, February 27). *3 things K-12 educators should know about the ethics and use of AI in education.* College of Education News. https://ced. ncsu.edu/news/2023/02/27/3-things-k-12-educators-should-know-about-the-ethics-and-use-of-ai-in-education/

Bravo, K. (2023, April 17). *How does AI actually work?* The Mozilla Blog. https://blog.mozilla.org/en/internet-culture/how-does-ai-work/

Briggs, S. (2014, February 1). *13 challenges for big data in education.* TeachThought. https://www.teachthought.com/the-future-of-learning/13-characteristics-data-rich-learning-environment/

Brown, C. (2019, July 25). *The history of personalized learning.* Classcraft Blog. https://www.classcraft.com/blog/the-history-of-personalized-learning/

Brown, M. (2023, May 30). *Student to teacher ratio in high schools.* Learner. https://www.learner.com/blog/student-to-teacher-ratio-in-high-schools

Brush, K., & Kirvan, P. (2019, December). *What is a learning management system (LMS) and what is it used for?* SearchCIO. https://www.techtarget.com/searchcio/definition/learning-management-system

*Build stronger connections with families.* (n.d.). ParentSquare. https://www.parentsquare.com/

Buluma Samba, Y. (2023, May 9). *AI technology "reduces stress for teachers and students."* TeachingTimes. https://www.teachingtimes.com/ai-technology-reduces-stress-for-teachers-and-students/

Burns, E. (2022, July 1). *What is artificial intelligence (AI)?* TechTarget; TechTarget. https://www.techtarget.com/searchenterpriseai/definition/AI-Artificial-Intelligence

Burns, M. (2023, March 15). *50 chatgpt prompts for teachers.* Class Tech Tips. https://classtechtips.com/2023/03/15/chatgpt-prompts-for-teachers/

Burton, C. (2023, April 26). *The role of AI in education.* Thinkific. https://www.thinkific.com/blog/ai-in-education/

Bushweller, K. (2019, November 5). Personalized learning: Challenges ahead, mistakes to avoid. *Education Week.* https://www.edweek.org/technology/personalized-learning-challenges-ahead-mistakes-to-avoid/2019/11

Campbell, R. (2023, March 13). *The right AI tools for your classroom.* Richard Campbell. https://richardccampbell.com/how-to-choose-the-right-ai-tools-for-your-classroom/

Cain, S. (2022, December 20). *A.I. is getting your holiday gifts to you more efficiently than ever.* Fortune. https://fortune.com/2022/12/20/tech-forward-everyday-ai-holiday-shipping-ups-fedex-amazon/

*Canva for Education: How to get started as a teacher*. (n.d.). Canva. https://www.canva.com/learn/canva-for-education/

Cardona, M. A., Rodriguez, R. J., & Ishmael, K. (2023). *Artificial intelligence and the future of teaching and learning insights and recommendations*. https://www2.ed.gov/documents/ai-report/ai-report.pdf

Chandra, S. (2021, July 13). *14 ways to gamify student engagement & learning*. CampusGroups. https://blog.campusgroups.com/campusgroups/2021/5/25/gamify-student-engagement-and-learning

Chapple, R. (2022, September 15). *Teacher burnout: a growing problem in schools*. Talkspace. https://www.talkspace.com/blog/teacher-burnout/

Chen, C. (2023, March 9). *AI will transform teaching and learning. let's get it right*. Stanford University HAI. https://hai.stanford.edu/news/ai-will-transform-teaching-and-learning-lets-get-it-right

Chernisky, C. (2023). *LibGuides: AI chatbots (ChatGPT): Teaching & learning: Avoiding plagiarism*. University of Hawaii James and Abigail Campbell Library. https://guides.westoahu.hawaii.edu/chatgpt/plagiarism

Chingos , M. M., & Whitehurst, G. J. (2011, May 11). *Class size: What research says and what it means for state policy*. Brookings Institution. https://www.brookings.edu/articles/class-size-what-research-says-and-what-it-means-for-state-policy/#_ftn7

Chorghe, K., Pawar, S., Sethy, G., & Pawar, V. (2021). AI based attendance monitoring system. *IJCRT, 9*(5), 2320–2882. https://www.ijcrt.org/papers/IJCRT2105287.pdf

Clairvoyant Perspectives. (2021, November 17). *Mining big data in education: Affordances and challenges*. Clairvoyant. https://www.clairvoyant.ai/blog/mining-big-data-in-education-affordances-and-challenges

Clark, H. (2023, August 6). *32 best AI chatbots for customer service in 2023*. The CX Lead. https://thecxlead.com/tools/best-ai-chatbot-for-customer-service/

*Classroom management strategies*. (n.d.). AI for Education. Retrieved November 28, 2023, from https://www.aiforeducation.io/prompt-library/classroom-management

*Classroom strategies to promote responsible use of A.I.* (n.d.). The Center for Teaching and Learning UNC Charlotte. https://teaching.charlotte.edu/teaching-support/teaching-guides/general-principles-teaching-age-ai

*Clive Humby*. (2021, July 12). Wikipedia. https://en.wikipedia.org/w/index.php?title=Clive_Humby&oldid=1160630515

*Consequences of mishandling sensitive data.* (2015, July 2). IT@Cornell. https://it. cornell.edu/security-and-policy/consequences-mishandling-sensitive-data

CooperGibson Research. (2023). *Exploring teachers' admin time.* United Kingdom Department of Education. https://assets.publishing.service.gov. uk/government/uploads/system/uploads/attachment_data/file/1171498/ Exploring_teachers__admin_time.pdf

Cortez, M. B. (2017, August 14). *Teachers struggle with personalized learning initiatives, study finds.* EdTech. https://edtechmagazine.com/k12/article/ 2017/08/teachers-struggle-personalized-learning-initiatives-study-finds

Council of Europe. (2014). *History of artificial intelligence.* Coe.int. https:// www.coe.int/en/web/artificial-intelligence/history-of-ai

Daley, S. (2018). *Surgical robots, new medicines and better care: 32 examples of AI in healthcare.* Built In. https://builtin.com/artificial-intelligence/artificial-intelligence-healthcare

Dani, V. (2019, January 2). *8 trends in education technology that will have A major impact.* Kitaboo. https://kitaboo.com/trends-in-education-technology/

Dené Poth, R. (2022, November 30). *How to avoid being overwhelmed by technology options.* Edutopia. https://www.edutopia.org/article/how-to-avoid-being-overwhelmed-by-technology-options/

Descant, S. (2021, May 5). *Los Angeles to install intelligent traffic signal controllers in hopes of improving safety.* GovTech. https://www.govtech.com/fs/los-angeles-to-install-intelligent-traffic-signal-controllers-in-hopes-of-improving-safety.html

Dodd, C. (n.d.). *Promoting academic integrity in the age of AI: Strategies for educators.* LINC. https://blog.linclearning.com/promoting-academic-integrity-in-the-age-of-ai-strategies-for-educators

Dodson, K. R. (2021, October 4). *Can gamification drive increased student engagement?* Educase Review. https://er.educause.edu/articles/sponsored/ 2021/10/can-gamification-drive-increased-student-engagement

Dutta, A. (2021, June 10). *Making personalized learning possible with AI.* Evelyn Learning. https://www.evelynlearning.com/using-ai-for-personalized-learning/

Earley, S. (n.d.). *Five myths about artificial intelligence.* TTEC. https://www.ttec. com/articles/five-myths-about-artificial-intelligence

Eaton, S. E. (2023, March 4). *Artificial intelligence and academic integrity, post-*

*plagiarism*. University World News. https://www.universityworldnews. com/post.php?story=20230228133041549

eclipse. (2020, October 5). *19 powerful ways to use artificial intelligence (AI) in ecommerce*. Linnworks

EdTech. (2019, March 19). *How AI in education saves time and encourages smarter decisions*. Cronofy. https://www.cronofy.com/blog/ai-education

Education Elements. (2017). *Six examples of what personalized learning looks like*. Education Elements. https://www.edelements.com/blog/six-examples-of-what-personalized-learning-looks-like

*8 benefits of using an AI-powered LMS*. (n.d.). SkillsYouNeed. Retrieved November 28, 2023, from https://www.skillsyouneed.com/rhubarb/ai-powered-lms.html

*Engagement management system for K-12 educators*. (2017). Classcraft. https:// www.classcraft.com/

*Epam*. (2020). Epam. https://www.epam.com/

*Ethical AI for teaching and learning*. (n.d.). Cornell Center for Teaching Innovation. https://teaching.cornell.edu/generative-artificial-intelligence/ ethical-ai-teaching-and-learning

Ewers, H. (2020, July 19). *The 20 biggest mistakes school communicators make & how to avoid them*. Badge Messenger. https://www.badgemessenger.com/ blog/school-communication-system.html

*Exploring 6 AI myths*. (n.d.). Google. https://ai.google/static/documents/explor ing-6-myths.pdf

*Find the best student engagement software*. (n.d.). Www.softwaresuggest.com. Retrieved November 28, 2023, from https://www.softwaresuggest.com/ student-engagement-software

*5 benefits of personalized learning*. (2022, September 27). 21K School. https:// www.21kschool.com/blog/5-benefits-of-personalized-learning/

Fontoura, J. (2023, July 31). *ChatGPT prompts to optimize your writing*. Rock Content. https://rockcontent.com/blog/optimize-writing-with-chatgpt-prompts/

Fourtane, S. (2022, December 16). Artificial intelligence in higher education: Benefits and ethics. *Fierce Education*. https://www.fierceeducation.com/ technology/artificial-intelligence-higher-education-benefits-and-ethics

Frąckiewicz, M. (2023a, May 3). *How AI is reshaping classroom management*. TS2 Space. https://ts2.space/en/how-ai-is-reshaping-classroom-management/

Frąckiewicz, M. (2023b, May 10). *AI in resource allocation*. TS2 Space. https://ts2.space/en/ai-in-resource-allocation/

Frąckiewicz, M. (2023c, June 25). *Fostering creativity in students: The role of AI*. TS2 Space. https://ts2.space/en/fostering-creativity-in-students-the-role-of-ai/

Frąckiewicz, M. (2023d, July 17). *The role of AI in streamlining administrative tasks in education*. TS2 SPACE. https://ts2.space/en/the-role-of-ai-in-streamlining-administrative-tasks-in-education/

Frankenfield, J. (2023, April 24). *Artificial intelligence: What it is and how it is used*. Investopedia. https://www.investopedia.com/terms/a/artificial-intelligence-ai.asp

Furze, L. (2023, January 26). *Teaching AI ethics*. Leon Furze. https://leonfurze.com/2023/01/26/teaching-ai-ethics/

Garner, I. (2023). *Data in education*. Learning A-Z. https://www.learninga-z.com/site/resources/breakroom-blog/data-in-education

George, A. (2023, May 31). *The importance of artificial intelligence in education for all students*. Language Magazine. https://www.languagemagazine.com/2023/05/31/the-importance-of-artificial-intelligence-in-education-for-all-students/

Gillis, A. (2022, May). *What is algorithm?* WhatIs.com. https://www.techtarget.com/whatis/definition/algorithm

Goff, J. (2023, February 26). *How a AI chatbot can improve teacher, student, and parent communication | artificial intelligence for teachers*. KDP Artificial Intelligence for Teachers. https://www.kdp.org/discussion/how-a-ai-chatbot-can-improve-teacher-student-and-parent-communication-1

GoGuardian Team. (2019, November 5). *Technology in the classroom | importance & challenges*. GoGuardian. https://www.goguardian.com/blog/technology-in-the-classroom-importance-challenges

Gravitas AI. (2023, May 16). *Future of AI in education: Trends for the next decade*. LinkedIn. https://www.linkedin.com/pulse/future-al-education-trends-next-decade-gravitas-ai

Gracious Quotes. "Top 33 Quotes About Artificial Intelligence." December 2, 2023. https://graciousquotes.com/artificial-intelligence/

Greenemeier, L. (2017, June 2). *20 years after deep blue: How AI has advanced since conquering chess*. Scientific American. https://www.scientificamerican.com/article/20-years-after-deep-blue-how-ai-has-advanced-since-conquering-chess/

Gupta, D. (2022, July 19). *AI applications and benefits in education sector.* Appinventiv. https://appinventiv.com/blog/10-ways-artificial-intelligence-transforming-the-education-industry/

Gupta, G. (2023, September 18). *The AI advantage: Boosting student engagement in self-paced learning through AI.* Faculty Focus. https://www.facultyfocus.com/articles/teaching-with-technology-articles/the-ai-advantage-boosting-student-engagement-in-self-paced-learning-through-ai/

Hardison, H. (2022, April 19). How teachers spend their time: A breakdown. *Education Week.* https://www.edweek.org/teaching-learning/how-teachers-spend-their-time-a-breakdown/2022/04

Hasib. (2023, June 15). *How to avoid plagiarism while using ChatGPT and AI tools.* GetGenie. https://getgenie.ai/how-to-avoid-plagiarism-with-ai-tools/

Henebery, B. (2023, March 10). *How AI chatbots are transforming school communication.* The Educator Australia. https://www.theeducatoronline.com/k12/news/how-ai-chatbots-are-transforming-school-communication/282137

Herold, B. (2017, November 8). *The case(s) against personalized learning.* Education Week. https://www.edweek.org/technology/the-cases-against-personalized-learning/2017/11

Herold, B. (2019, November 6). *What is personalized learning?* Education Week. https://www.edweek.org/technology/what-is-personalized-learning/2019/11

*History of artificial intelligence.* (2014). Council of Europe. https://www.coe.int/en/web/artificial-intelligence/history-of-ai

*Homepage.* (n.d.). BrightBytes. https://www.brightbytes.net/

*How can AI help address the global challenges and opportunities in education?* (n.d.). LinkedIn. Retrieved November 28, 2023, from https://www.linkedin.com/advice/0/how-can-ai-help-address-global-challenges

*How do you ensure data privacy and security when using AI for adaptive learning?* (n.d.). LinkedIn. Retrieved November 28, 2023, from https://www.linkedin.com/advice/0/how-do-you-ensure-data-privacy-security-when

*How do you keep up with the latest trends and innovations in AI?* (n.d.). LinkedIn. Retrieved November 28, 2023, from https://www.linkedin.com/advice/3/how-do-you-keep-up-latest-trends-innovations-7041842070671556608

*How do you manage and store educational data in a way that is accessible, reliable, and scalable?* (n.d.). LinkedIn. https://www.linkedin.com/advice/0/how-do-you-manage-store-educational-data-way-accessible

*How do you use data and evidence to inform resource allocation decisions in education?* (n.d.). LinkedIn. Retrieved November 28, 2023, from https://www. linkedin.com/advice/1/how-do-you-use-data-evidence-inform-resource

*How schools can use artificial intelligence to reduce teachers' workload.* (2023, May 15). Teaching Personnel. https://www.teachingpersonnel.com/tp-posts/ 2023-5/using-ai-to-reduce-teachers-workload

*How to recognise and manage teacher burnout.* (n.d.). ReachOut. https://schools. au.reachout.com/articles/how-to-recognise-and-manage-teacher-burnout

*How to use AI in the classroom.* (n.d.). @TheMerrillsEDU. https://www.themer rillsedu.com/blog-1/2023/2/17/how-to-use-ai-in-the-classroom

Hryshkevich, H. (2022, September 14). *5 ways we use AI without knowing about it.* AI Time Journal - Artificial Intelligence, Automation, Work and Business. https://www.aitimejournal.com/how-we-use-ai-without-know ing-about-it/

Hyndman, B. (2018). Ten reasons why teachers can struggle to use technology in the classroom. *Science Educational News, 67.* https://researchoutput.csu. edu.au/ws/portalfiles/portal/124325978/34366631_Published_arti

IBM Education. (2023, July 11). *The benefits of AI in healthcare.* IBM Blog. https://www.ibm.com/blog/the-benefits-of-ai-in-healthcare/

Impey, C., & Formanek, M. (2021). MOOCS and 100 Days of COVID: Enrollment surges in massive open online astronomy classes during the coronavirus pandemic. *Social Sciences & Humanities Open, 4*(1), 100177. https://doi.org/10.1016/j.ssaho.2021.100177

*Interactive Learning: The benefits of engaging students in their education.* (n.d.). Sendsteps. Retrieved November 28, 2023, from https://www.sendsteps. com/en/blog/interactive-learning-the-benefits-of-engaging-students-in-their-education/

Israrkhan. (2021, June 24). *Top 10 struggles teachers face to integrate technology in the classroom.* Illumination; Medium. https://medium.com/illumination/ top-10-struggles-teachers-face-to-integrate-technology-in-the-class room-51d9693dbf5f

Jenkins, A., & Kelly, C. (2016). *Biggest challenges in personalized learning fall 2016.* Education Elements. https://www.edelements.com/hubfs/ Education_Elements_Biggest_Challenges_in_Personalized_Learning_ Analysis_2016.pdf

Johnson, M. (2022, May 24). *AI in eCommerce: Benefits and examples.*

Www.divante.com. https://www.divante.com/blog/ai-in-ecommerce-benefits-and-examples

Johnsrud , B. (2023, September 27). *How to drive student success with creative generative AI tools in the classroom: Part 1 - edsurge news*. EdSurge. https://www.edsurge.com/news/2023-09-27-how-to-drive-student-success-with-creative-generative-ai-tools-in-the-classroom-part-1

Joseph. (2022, December 21). *How to avoid plagiarism while using ChatGPT in writing your essays*. Plagexpert. https://www.plagexpert.com/how-to-avoid-plagiarism-while-using-chatgpt-in-writing-your-essays/

Joshi, N. (2022, November 15). *Why using AI in education could be a game changer*. Allerin. https://www.allerin.com/blog/why-using-ai-in-education-could-be-a-game-changer

K, M. (2023, June 6). *How AI is personalizing education for every student*. ELearning Industry. https://elearningindustry.com/how-ai-is-personalizing-education-for-every-student

Kahoot! (2019, June 5). *Kahoot! For schools*. Kahoot! https://kahoot.com/schools/

Keserer, E. (2022, December 5). *The five main subsets of AI: (Machine learning, NLP, and more)*. Akkio. https://www.akkio.com/post/the-five-main-subsets-of-ai-machine-learning-nlp-and-more

Kim, E. T. (2019, July 10). The messy reality of personalized learning. *The New Yorker*. https://www.newyorker.com/news/dispatch/the-messy-reality-of-personalized-learning

Kolesnikova, I. (2023, January 15). *How AI in transportation can improve our everyday lives*. MindTitan. https://mindtitan.com/resources/blog/ai-in-transportation/

Kompella, K. (2022, September 27). *The pros and cons of using AI-based mental health tools*. Information Today. https://newsbreaks.infotoday.com/NewsBreaks/The-Pros-and-Cons-of-Using-AIBased-Mental-Health-Tools-155090.asp

Krishnan, J. (2023, June 9). *Exploring the pros and cons of AI in mental health care*. Active Minds. https://www.activeminds.org/blog/exploring-the-pros-and-cons-of-ai-in-mental-health-care/

Kumar, A. (2022, April 20). *How are eLearning solutions becoming better with AI paper graders?* ELearning Industry. https://elearningindustry.com/how-are-elearning-solutions-becoming-better-with-ai-paper-graders

Kumar, M. (2022, April 18). *Importance of artificial intelligence in transportation*.

Aeologic Blog. https://www.aeologic.com/blog/importance-of-artificial-intelligence-in-transportation/

Kumar, R. (2023). Faculty members' use of artificial intelligence to grade student papers: a case of implications. *International Journal for Educational Integrity, 19*(1). https://doi.org/10.1007/s40979-023-00130-7

Ladd, H. F., Hemelt, S. W., & Clifton, C. R. (2021, August 24). *Teacher assistants are needed—now more than ever.* Brookings. https://www.brookings.edu/articles/teacher-assistants-are-needed-now-more-than-ever/

Langreo, L. (2023a, March 6). How to use artificial intelligence to bolster students' creativity. *Education Week.* https://www.edweek.org/technology/how-to-use-artificial-intelligence-to-bolster-students-creativity/2023/03

Langreo, L. (2023b, June 27). 7 strategies to prepare educators to teach with AI. *Education Week.* https://www.edweek.org/teaching-learning/7-strate gies-to-prepare-educators-to-teach-with-ai/2023/06

Lateef, Z. (2019, June 18). *Types of artificial intelligence you should know.* Edureka. https://www.edureka.co/blog/types-of-artificial-intelligence/

*Learning management.* (n.d.). Anthology Blackboard Learn. Retrieved November 28, 2023, from https://www.anthology.com/discover/anthol ogy-learning-management/

Lehmann, J. (2023, August 14). *Research shows extensive use of AI contains data breaches faster and saves significant costs.* IBM Blog. https://www.ibm.com/blog/research-shows-extensive-use-of-ai-contains-data-breaches-faster-and-saves-significant-costs/

Li, J., Xiao, W., & Zhang, C. (2023). Data security crisis in universities: identi-fication of key factors affecting data breach incidents. *Humanities & Social Sciences Communications, 10*(1), 270. https://doi.org/10.1057/s41599-023-01757-0

Lieberman, M. (2022, June 27). 3 strategies for helping students navigate the ethics of artificial intelligence. *Education Week.* https://www.edweek.org/technology/3-strategies-for-helping-students-navigate-the-ethics-of-arti ficial-intelligence/2022/06

Llego, M. A. (2023, March 22). *Adapting to AI in education: Strategies for encour-aging critical thinking and human connection in the classroom.* TeacherPH. https://www.teacherph.com/adapting-ai-education-strategies-critical-thinking-human-connection/

Lutkevich, B. (2023, January). *What are self-driving cars and how do they work?*

TechTarget. https://www.techtarget.com/searchenterpriseai/definition/driverless-car

Lynch, M. (2019, October 21). *Using machine learning to modify student behavior.* The Tech Edvocate. https://www.thetechedvocate.org/using-machine-learning-to-modify-student-behavior/

Lynch, M. (2021, December 30). Why are some educators still reluctant to use technology in the classroom? *Thetechedvocate.org.* https://www.thetechedvocate.org/why-are-some-educators-still-reluctant-to-use-technology-in-the-classroom/

Madrid, R. B. (2020, January 16). *Teaching with limited resources: challenges and potential benefits.* TEFL Trainer. https://tefltrainer.com/general/teaching-limited-resources-challenges-potential-benefits/

Maffea, J. (2020). *Lack of resources in classrooms lack of resources in classrooms.* https://research.library.kutztown.edu/cgi/viewcontent.cgi?article=1003&context=wickedproblems

*Make learning fun, adaptive and insightful.* (n.d.). Prodigy. https://www.prodigygame.com/main-en/teachers/

Makieiev, E. (n.d.). *9 benefits of artificial intelligence (AI) in the transportation industry and related fields | Integrio Systems Blog.* Integrio Systems. https://integrio.net/blog/benefits-of-artificial-intelligence

Manyika, J., Lund, S., Chui, M., Bughin, J., Woetzel, J., Batra, P., Ko, R., & Sanghvi, S. (2017). *Jobs lost, jobs gained: What the future of work will mean for jobs, skills, and wages.* McKinsey & Company. https://www.mckinsey.com/featured-insights/future-of-work/jobs-lost-jobs-gained-what-the-future-of-work-will-mean-for-jobs-skills-and-wages

Marr, B. (2019, December 16). *The 10 best examples of how AI is already used in our everyday life.* Forbes. https://www.forbes.com/sites/bernardmarr/2019/12/16/the-10-best-examples-of-how-ai-is-already-used-in-our-everyday-life/

Martin, A. (2021, May 19). *Using interactive learning to improve student engagement.* TeachHUB. https://www.teachhub.com/professional-development/2021/05/using-interactive-learning-to-improve-student-engagement/

Mazo, J. (2023, May 17). *Protecting student privacy: Safeguarding data security in the age of AI technology.* LinkedIn. https://www.linkedin.com/pulse/protecting-student-privacy-safeguarding-data-security-john-mazo

McFarland, A. (2022, March 31). *10 best AI tools for education.* Unite.AI. https://www.unite.ai/10-best-ai-tools-for-education/

McKean, J. (2022). *7 steps for making data-driven decisions in education*. PowerSchool. https://www.powerschool.com/blog/7-steps-for-making-data-driven-decision-in-education/

McKinsey & Company. (2023, April 24). *What is AI?* Www.mckinsey.com. https://www.mckinsey.com/featured-insights/mckinsey-explainers/what-is-ai

McNamee, J. (2022, December 14). *Erica becomes a little more human*. Insider Intelligence. https://www.insiderintelligence.com/content/bank-of-america-adds-human-touch-erica

McSpadden, K. (2015, May 14). *You now have a shorter attention span than a goldfish*. Time. https://time.com/3858309/attention-spans-goldfish/

Mead, S. (n.d.). *Differentiated learning: Why "one size fits all" doesn't work in education*. Whitby School. Retrieved November 28, 2023, from https://www.whitbyschool.org/passionforlearning/differentiated-learning-why-one-size-fits-all-doesnt-work-in-education

*Meet Socrative*. (2022). Socrative. https://www.socrative.com/

Metz, C. (2016, January 25). *The rise of the artificially intelligent hedge fund*. Wired. https://www.wired.com/2016/01/the-rise-of-the-artificially-intelligent-hedge-fund/

*More effective, engaging learning — from anywhere*. (2014). GoGuardian. https://www.goguardian.com/

Morin, A. (2022). *What is personalized learning*. Understood. https://www.understood.org/en/articles/personalized-learning-what-you-need-to-know

Moroz, A. (2022, September 30). *Burnout in tech: What causes it and how to deal with it*. LinkedIn. https://www.linkedin.com/pulse/burnout-tech-what-causes-how-deal-anna-moroz

Morris, S. (2023, June 22). *ChatGPT alternatives: 31 AI tools teachers should know about*. We Are Teachers. https://www.weareteachers.com/chatgpt-alternatives/

Mosier, A. (2018). *ScholarWorks teachers' challenges in implementing personalized learning in content areas*. https://scholarworks.waldenu.edu/cgi/viewcontent.cgi?article=7187&context=dissertations

Munagapati, S. (2023, October 3). *The impact of artificial intelligence on e-commerce: Everything you need to know*. https://www.sellerapp.com/blog/artificial-intelligence-ai-e-commerce/

*Nearpod | technology in the classroom*. (2018). Nearpod. https://nearpod.com/

Nield, D. (2023, July 23). *5 ways ChatGPT can improve, not replace, your writing.* Wired UK. https://www.wired.co.uk/article/chatgpt-writing-tips

O'Rourke, S. (2022, January 25). *6 benefits of personalized learning.* RingCentral. https://www.ringcentral.com/us/en/blog/benefits-personalized-learning/

Ofgang, E. (2023, April 24). *10 AI tools beyond chatgpt that can save teachers time.* Tech Learning Magazine. https://www.techlearning.com/news/10-ai-tools-beyond-chatgpt-that-can-save-teachers-time

*One size doesn't fit all in education.* (2020, June 5). Education Evolution. https://educationevolution.org/one-size-doesnt-fit-all/

Ortiz, S. (2023, September 15). How to use ChatGPT to write an essay. *ZDNet.* https://www.zdnet.com/article/how-to-use-chatgpt-to-write-an-essay/

Otte, S. (2018, December 28). *How does Artificial Intelligence work?* Innoplexus. https://www.innoplexus.com/blog/how-artificial-intelligence-works/

Overby, S. (2020, May 7). *5 artificial intelligence (AI) types, defined.* Enterprisers Project. https://enterprisersproject.com/article/2020/5/5-artificial-intelligence-ai-types-defined

Pappas, C. (2022, October 23). *6 obstacles that stand in the way of student engagement.* ELearning Industry. https://elearningindustry.com/obstacles-that-stand-in-the-way-of-student-engagement

Pardo, L. (2023, June 26). *5 ethical implications of AI in education: A guideline for responsible classroom implementation.* Quizalize Blog . https://blog.quizalize.com/2023/06/26/5-ethical-implications-of-ai-in-education/

*Personalized learning: Plan, benefits, examples.* (2023, June 17). Valamis. https://www.valamis.com/hub/personalized-learning

Plesner, L. L. (2023, March 7). *AI accurately identifies normal and abnormal chest x-rays.* Www.rsna.org. https://www.rsna.org/news/2023/march/ai-identifies-normal-abnormal-xrays

Plitnichenko, L. (2020, May 30). *5 main roles of artificial intelligence in education.* ELearning Industry. https://elearningindustry.com/5-main-roles-artificial-intelligence-in-education

*Plotagon Story.* (n.d.). Plotagon. https://www.plotagon.com/

Positive Action Staff. (2021, April 30). *6 behavior management strategies for your classroom in 2021.* Positive Action. https://www.positiveaction.net/blog/behavior-management-strategies

Processica. (2023, August 14). *Generative AI step-by-step guide for educators.*

LinkedIn. https://www.linkedin.com/pulse/generative-ai-step-by-step-guide-educators-processica

Professor Synapse. (2023, May 15). *Navigating AI ethics in education.* Synaptic Labs. https://blog.synapticlabs.ai/education/navigating-ai-ethics-in-education

Prothero, A. (2023, June 20). *Educators starting to incorporate AI into regular tasks.* GovTech. https://www.govtech.com/education/k-12/educators-starting-to-incorporate-ai-into-regular-tasks

Q.ai. (2023, January 6). Applications of artificial intelligence across various industries. *Forbes.* https://www.forbes.com/sites/qai/2023/01/06/applications-of-artificial-intelligence/

Qiu, Y., Pan, J., & Ishak, N. A. (2022). Effectiveness of artificial intelligence (AI) in improving pupils' deep learning in primary school mathematics teaching in fujian province. *Computational Intelligence and Neuroscience, 2022,* 1–10. https://doi.org/10.1155/2022/1362996

Quinn, C. (2021, June 29). *Screaming in the cloud* (225: Burnout Isn't a Sign of Weakness with Dr. Christina Maslach, PhD) [Podcast]. Last Week in AWS.

Raath, S. (2023, April 17). *How to improve your writing with ChatGPT.* Express VPN. https://www.expressvpn.com/blog/guide-how-to-use-chatgpt-to-improve-your-writing/

Rademaker, R. (2023, April 6). *New AI technology supports teachers - Creating exams will never be the same with Dugga's new innovation.* Dugga. https://dugga.com/new-ai-technology-supports-teachers-creating-exams-will-never-be-the-same-with-duggas-new-innovation/

Raturi, A. (2023, May 15). *How AI is helping teachers improve classroom management?* Igebra.ai. https://www.igebra.ai/blog/how-ai-is-helping-teachers-improve-classroom-management/

Ravaglia, R. (2023, March 25). *Student engagement matters more than attendance; why don't schools track it?* Forbes. https://www.forbes.com/sites/rayravaglia/2023/03/25/student-engagement-matters-more-than-atten dance-why-dont-schools-track-it/?sh=2e7426d77811

Reber, R., Canning, E. A., & Harackiewicz, J. M. (2018). Personalized education to increase interest. *Current Directions in Psychological Science, 27*(6), 449–454. https://doi.org/10.1177/0963721418793140

*Resource of the month.* (n.d.). AI for Teachers. Retrieved November 28, 2023, from https://www.aiforteachers.org/featured-resource

Rizzoli, A. (2021, December 9). *AI in transportation: 9 disruptive use cases [2022 update]*. V7 Labs. https://www.v7labs.com/blog/ai-in-transportation

Roser, M. (2022, December 6). *The brief history of artificial intelligence: The world has changed fast – what might be next?* Our World in Data. https://ourworldindata.org/brief-history-of-ai

Ross, E. (2023, July 20). *Embracing artificial intelligence in the classroom*. Harvard Graduate School of Education. https://www.gse.harvard.edu/ideas/usable-knowledge/23/07/embracing-artificial-intelligence-classroom

Ross, O. (2022, December 31). *AI for authors: Practical and ethical guidelines*. Self-Publishing Advice Center from the Alliance of Independent Authors. https://selfpublishingadvice.org/ai-for-authors-guidelines/

Rouhiainen, L. (2019, October 14). *How AI and data could personalize higher education*. Harvard Business Review. https://hbr.org/2019/10/how-ai-and-data-could-personalize-higher-education

Rutner, S., & Scott, R. (2022). *Use of artificial intelligence to grade student discussion boards: An exploratory study*. https://files.eric.ed.gov/fulltext/EJ1358299.pdf

Ryan, E. (2023, June 29). *Is using ChatGPT cheating?* Scribbr. https://www.scribbr.com/ai-tools/chatgpt-cheating/

Sanjeewa, K. (2022, April 5). *5 tips to help teachers with data-driven decision making*. OctopusBI. https://octopusbi.com/5-tips-to-help-teachers-with-data-driven-decision-making/

Sarwar, A. (2023, March 9). *The rise of AI in mental health: Pros, cons, and ethical considerations*. LinkedIn. https://www.linkedin.com/pulse/rise-ai-mental-health-pros-cons-ethical-adeel-sarwar

Satpute, N., Bharti, N., Uikey, A., Wati, R., & Chakole, Vijay. V. (2022). Online classroom attendance marking system using face recognition, python, computer vision, and digital image processing. *International Journal for Research in Applied Science and Engineering Technology, 10*(2), 768–773. https://doi.org/10.22214/ijraset.2022.40356

Sauber Millacci, T. (2021, November 11). Teacher burnout: 4 warning signs & how to prevent it. *Positivepsychology.* https://positivepsychology.com/teacher-burnout/

Schifter, C. C., Natarajan, U., Jass Ketelhut, D., & Kirchgessner, A. (n.d.). *Data-Driven decision making: Facilitating teacher use of student data to inform classroom instruction – CITE journal*. Contemporary Issues in Technology and Teacher Education, 14(4). https://citejournal.org/volume-14/issue-4-14/

science/data-driven-decision-making-facilitating-teacher-use-of-student-data-to-inform-classroom-instruction

*School inventory management software.* (n.d.). Sortly. Retrieved November 28, 2023, from https://www.sortly.com/industries/education-inventory-management-software/

*School inventory system and asset tracking.* (n.d.). ASAP Systems. Retrieved November 28, 2023, from https://asapsystems.com/education/

Schroer, A. (2019). *AI and the bottom line: 15 examples of artificial intelligence in finance.* Built In. https://builtin.com/artificial-intelligence/ai-finance-banking-applications-companies

Schroer, A. (2023, July 27). *What is artificial intelligence? How does AI work?* Builtin. https://builtin.com/artificial-intelligence

Scott , C. (2023, June 28). *Adapt or die part 2: Top 20 things educators must do to stay relevant in the age of AI.* LinkedIn. https://www.linkedin.com/pulse/adapt-die-part-2-top-20-things-educators-must-do-stay-cory-scott

*Selected characteristics of public school teachers: Selected years, spring 1961 through spring 2006.* (2010, June). Nces.ed.gov. https://nces.ed.gov/programs/digest/d12/tables/dt12_081.asp

Seo, K., Tang, J., Roll, I., Fels, S., & Yoon, D. (2021). The impact of artificial intelligence on learner–instructor interaction in online learning. *International Journal of Educational Technology in Higher Education, 18*(1). https://doi.org/10.1186/s41239-021-00292-9

*17 best AI tools for students (2023).* (2023). Edarabia. https://www.edarabia.com/17-best-ai-tools-students/

Shabbir, R. (2023, May 4). *9 Must-Have AI Tools for Teachers to Create Interactive Learning Materials.* Educationise. https://www.educationise.com/post/9-must-have-ai-tools-for-teachers-to-enhance-classroom-experience

Shopify Staff. (2023, June 13). *AI in ecommerce: Applications, benefits, and challenges.* Shopify. https://www.shopify.com/blog/ai-ecommerce

*6 AI myths debunked.* (2019, November 5). Gartner. https://www.gartner.com/smarterwithgartner/5-ai-myths-debunked

*60 top AI personalized learning platform tools.* (n.d.). TopAI.tools. https://topai.tools/s/personalized-learning-platform

Smith, A. (2023, April 12). *What is the role of artificial intelligence in education?* Acade Craft. https://www.acadecraft.com/blog/role-of-artificial-intelligence-in-education-and-learning/

Spacey, J. (2021, September 3). *56 examples of student data*. Simplicable. https://simplicable.com/edu/student-data

Staff, S. (2023, June 13). *AI in ecommerce: Applications, benefits, and challenges.* Shopify. https://www.shopify.com/blog/ai-ecommerce

Stone, A. (2021, September 13). *Can artificial intelligence help prevent teacher burnout?* Emerging Education Technologies. https://www.emergingedtech.com/2021/09/can-artificial-intelligence-help-prevent-teacher-burnout/

*Student engagement platform software with monitoring.* (n.d.). GetApp. https://www.getapp.com/education-childcare-software/student-engagement-platform/f/monitoring/

Suarez-Davis , J. (2022, December 12). *Data isn't "the new oil" - it's way more valuable than that.* The Drum. https://www.thedrum.com/opinion/2022/12/12/data-isn-t-the-new-oil-it-s-way-more-valuable

Sutton, E. (2021). *Student engagement: Why it's important and how to promote it.* Branching Minds. https://www.branchingminds.com/blog/student-engagement-remote-in-person

Sutty, S. (2018, April 6). *Five advantages of personalized learning.* Sanford School. https://blogs.sanfordschool.org/five-advantages-of-personalized-learning

Sweet, K. (2023, August 28). *How PayPal is using AI to combat fraud, and make it easier to pay.* AP News. https://apnews.com/article/paypal-artificial-intelligence-payments-security-cybersecurity-96ce016ed5ac2aad76bda6b778e1fd0f

Tapp, F. (2019, November 12). *Teacher burnout: Causes, symptoms, and prevention.* Hey Teach!; Western Governors University. https://www.wgu.edu/heyteach/article/teacher-burnout-causes-symptoms-and-prevention1711.html

*Teacher burnout and how to avoid it.* (2023). Education Support. https://www.educationsupport.org.uk/resources/for-individuals/articles/teacher-burnout-and-how-to-avoid-it/

*Teacher demographics and statistics: Number of teachers in the US.* (2021, January 29). Zippia. https://www.zippia.com/teacher-jobs/demographics/

*Teaching AI: Educator resources for artificial intelligence in the...* (n.d.). Intel. https://www.intel.com/content/www/us/en/education/k12/teachers/teaching-ai.html

*Teaching with limited resources: challenges and potential benefits.* (2020, January

16). TEFL Trainer. https://tefltrainer.com/general/teaching-limited-resources-challenges-potential-benefits/

*10 free AI tools for teachers to create engaging lessons and boost student achievement - igebra.* (2023, May 3). Igebra.ai. https://www.igebra.ai/blog/10-free-ai-tools-for-teachers-to-create-engaging-lessons-and-boost-student-achievement/

Tenenbaum, J. S. (2023, April 27). *Five key legal issues to consider when it comes to generative AI.* ASAE. https://www.asaecenter.org/resources/articles/an_plus/2023/4-april/five-key-legal-issues-to-consider-when-it-comes-to-ai

Tessler, H. (2023, March 25). *How AI changing cybersecurity landscape in education.* Hans India. https://www.thehansindia.com/hans/young-hans/how-ai-changing-cybersecurity-landscape-in-education-789521

*The benefits of personalized learning.* (n.d.). Learning Lab. Retrieved November 28, 2023, from https://mylearnlab.com/articles/the-benefits-of-personalized-learning/

*The different types of data in education: A complete guide.* (2023, May 10). Innovare. https://innovaresip.com/resources/blog/types-of-data-in-education/

*The ethics of AI in education:* (2023, June 5). Taxila Business School. https://taxila.in/blog/the-ethics-of-ai-in-education/

*The importance of artificial intelligence in education for all students.* (2023, May 31). Language Magazine. https://www.languagemagazine.com/2023/05/31/the-importance-of-artificial-intelligence-in-education-for-all-students/

*The smartest way to prevent student harm.* (n.d.). Navigate 360. Retrieved December 5, 2023, from https://info.navigate360.com/smartest-way-prevent-student-harm

The Upwork Team. (6 C.E.). *How does AI work? Fundamentals and step-by-step process.* Upwork. https://www.upwork.com/resources/how-does-ai-work

*30 AI tools for the classroom.* (2023, May 2). Ditch That Textbook. https://ditchthattextbook.com/ai-tools/

*31 incredible AI tools for education you need to try right now!* . (2023, February 21). Eklavvya. https://www.eklavvya.com/blog/ai-edtech-tools/

Thomas, R. (2023, August 11). *Generative AI ethics in academic writing.* Enago Academy. https://www.enago.com/academy/generative-ai-ethics-in-academic-writing/

ThorimAI. (2023, September 19). *How AI can alleviate teacher burnout* . LinkedIn. https://www.linkedin.com/pulse/how-ai-can-alleviate-teacher-burnout-thorimai

*Tips, guidance, and resources for instructors to adapt to AI in the classroom.* (2023, August 7). University of Iowa Office of the Executive Vice President and Provost. https://provost.uiowa.edu/news/2023/08/tips-guidance-and-resources-instructors-adapt-ai-classroom

Torchia , R. (2022, February 22). *The checklist: 5 steps to secure student data.* Technology Solutions That Drive Education. https://edtechmagazine.com/k12/article/2022/02/checklist-5-steps-secure-student-data

Trabelsi, Z., Alnajjar, F., Parambil, M. M. A., Gochoo, M., & Ali, L. (2023). Real-Time attention monitoring system for classroom: A deep learning approach for student's behavior recognition. *Big Data and Cognitive Computing, 7*(1), 48. https://doi.org/10.3390/bdcc7010048

Treece, K. (2023, July 6). *Upstart vs. LendingClub: Which one is best for you?* Forbes Advisor. https://www.forbes.com/advisor/personal-loans/upstart-vs-lendingclub/

*20 best student engagement software for 2023.* (n.d.). Software Suggest. https://www.softwaresuggest.com/student-engagement-software

University of San Diego. (2021, April 2). *Artificial intelligence in finance [15 examples].* University of San Diego. https://onlinedegrees.sandiego.edu/artificial-intelligence-finance/

*Using data to improve the quality of education.* (2023). Unesco IIEP Learning Portal. https://learningportal.iiep.unesco.org/en/issue-briefs/monitor-learning/using-data-to-improve-the-quality-of-education

V K , A. (2022, February 10). *10 most common myths about AI.* Spiceworks. https://www.spiceworks.com/tech/artificial-intelligence/articles/common-myths-about-ai/

Verbit Editorial. (2021, March 16). *Artificial intelligence in education: Present and future of intelligence.* Verbit. https://verbit.ai/artificial-intelligence-in-education/

Volyntseva, Y. (2022, July 13). *How artificial intelligence is used for data analytics.* Business Tech Weekly. https://www.businesstechweekly.com/operational-efficiency/data-management/how-artificial-intelligence-is-used-for-data-analytics/

Walley, M. (2023, February 1). *Teachers are burning out. Can AI help?* ESchool

News. https://www.eschoolnews.com/digital-learning/2023/02/01/teach ers-are-burning-out-can-ai-help/

Walsh, D. (2023, August 30). *The legal issues presented by generative AI.* MIT Sloan. https://mitsloan.mit.edu/ideas-made-to-matter/legal-issues-presented-generative-ai

Wang, H., Gao, C., Hong, F., Zong-Hao, C., Wang, Q., He, Z., & Li, M. (2023). Automated student classroom behaviors' perception and identification using motion sensors. *Bioengineering, 10*(2), 127–127. https://doi.org/10.3390/bioengineering10020127

Watson, A. (n.d.). *10 tips for avoiding technology overwhelm.* Truth for Teachers. https://truthforteachers.com/truth-for-teachers-podcast/10-tips-avoid ing-technology-overwhelm/

Welding, L. (2023, March 27). *Half of college students say using AI is cheating.* Best Colleges. https://www.bestcolleges.com/research/college-students-ai-tools-survey/

Wen, A. (2023, February 13). *The freakout over ChatGPT and cheating may be misguided.* Teen Vogue. https://www.teenvogue.com/story/chatgpt-plagia rism-cheating-students

*What are the benefits and challenges of using data-driven decision making in educa-tion?* (n.d.). LinkedIn. Retrieved November 28, 2023, from https://www.linkedin.com/advice/0/what-benefits-challenges-using-data-driven-3e

*What are the current trends and future directions of artificial intelligence in educa-tion research?* (n.d.). LinkedIn. Retrieved November 28, 2023, from https://www.linkedin.com/advice/1/what-current-trends-future-directions-artificial

*What is AI?* (2023, April 24). McKinsey & Company. https://www.mckinsey.com/featured-insights/mckinsey-explainers/what-is-ai

*What is artificial intelligence (AI)?* (2023). IBM. https://www.ibm.com/topics/artificial-intelligence

*What is the history of artificial intelligence (AI)?* (n.d.). Salesforce Tableau. https://www.tableau.com/data-insights/ai/history

*What is the most creative way to use AI in the classroom?* (2023, August 26). Reddit. https://www.reddit.com/r/education/comments/161y4bx/what_is_the_most_creative_way_to_use_ai_in_the/

*Where classrooms become communities.* (2019). ClassDojo. https://www.classdojo.com/

*Why do some teachers take so long to put in grades?* (2019). Quora. https://www.quora.com/Why-do-some-teachers-take-so-long-to-put-in-grades

Wilson, C. (2023, April 4). *How AI works: The basics you need to know.* Hub Spot Blog. https://blog.hubspot.com/marketing/how-does-ai-work

Wong, J. (2023, May 23). *Fostering creativity and critical thinking with AI in education.* SpacesEDU. https://spacesedu.com/en/fostering-creativity-and-critical-thinking-with-ai-in-education/

Zhao, M., Zhao, G., & Qu, M. (2022). College smart classroom attendance management system based on internet of things. *Computational Intelligence and Neuroscience, 2022,* 1–9. https://doi.org/10.1155/2022/4953721

Zia, T. (2023, July 19). *Transforming Education: AI-Powered Personalized Learning Revolution.* Techopedia. https://www.techopedia.com/transforming-education-ai-powered-personalized-learning-revolution

Made in the USA
Monee, IL
11 December 2024

73016052R00105